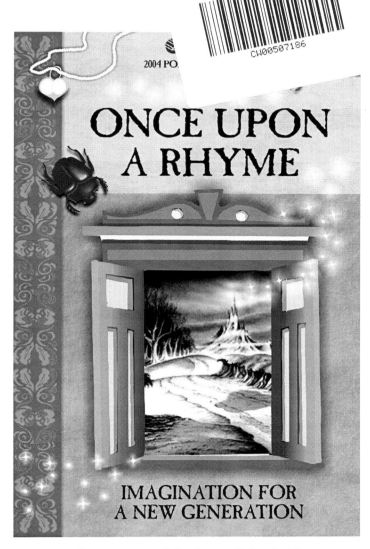

2004 PO.

ONCE UPON A RHYME

IMAGINATION FOR A NEW GENERATION

South Wales Vol II
Edited by Steve Twelvetree

 Young**Writers**

First published in Great Britain in 2004 by:
Young Writers
Remus House
Coltsfoot Drive
Peterborough
PE2 9JX
Telephone: 01733 890066
Website: www.youngwriters.co.uk

SB ISBN 1 84460 589 2

Foreword

Young Writers was established in 1991 and has been passionately devoted to the promotion of reading and writing in children and young adults ever since. The quest continues today. Young Writers remains as committed to engendering the fostering of burgeoning poetic and literary talent as ever.

This year's Young Writers competition has proven as vibrant and dynamic as ever and we are delighted to present a showcase of the best poetry from across the UK. Each poem has been carefully selected from a wealth of *Once Upon A Rhyme* entries before ultimately being published in this, our twelfth primary school poetry series.

Once again, we have been supremely impressed by the overall high quality of the entries we have received. The imagination, energy and creativity which has gone into each young writer's entry made choosing the best poems a challenging and often difficult but ultimately hugely rewarding task - the general high standard of the work submitted amply vindicating this opportunity to bring their poetry to a larger appreciative audience.

We sincerely hope you are pleased with our final selection and that you will enjoy *Once Upon A Rhyme South Wales Vol II* for many years to come.

Contents

Bethanne Evans (9)   14
James Sell (10)   15
Jordan Dawson (10)   15
Jordan Day (8)   15
Joshua Weir (10)   16

Derwendeg Primary School, Hengoed
Luke Wood (10)   16
Ieuan Elliot (9)   16
Sarah Fisher (10)   17
Sasha Paget (10)   17
Sarah Greenslade (9)   17
Ashlee Matthews (10)   18
Kodie Mackay (9)   18
Emily James (9)   18
Amy Baker (10)   19
Matthew Jay (9)   19
Paige Sanders (10)   19
Sadie Thomas (10)   20
Carly Osborne (9)   20
Amber Roberts (9)   20
Jade Jones (9)   21
Sasha Kumar (9)   21
Rhys Spanswick (9)   21
Abbi Parker (9)   22
Lewis Green (10)   22
Nicole Fox (10)   22
Shauna Day (10)   23
Rhys Carroll (10)   23
Ashley Dwyer (9)   23
Danial Huxter (9)   24
Katie Aldridge (9)   24
Joe Williams (9)   24
Lauren Dickens (9)   25
Lauren Emmett (9)   25
Chelsea Hayes (9)   25
Tabitha Hughes (9)   26
Belinda Nelmes (9)   26
Lucy Burke (9)   26
Geraint Dallimore (9)   27
Jack Wood (9)   27

Durham Road Junior School, Newport

Zoey Mitchell (10)	27
Ayesha Behit (10)	28
Kaidie-Jae Prytherch (8)	28
Rukhsar Hanif (11)	29
Chloe Pickering (10)	29
George McDonagh (8)	30
Carmen Goodyear (9)	30
Curtis Jones (8)	31
Daniel Buttigieg & Jake Sicolo (10)	31
Sheridan Lacey (11)	32
Declan Henry (9)	32
Alice Sayle (9)	33
Jessica Moore (11)	33
Hollie Kehoe (11)	34
Chelsea Powell	34
Ryan Perkin (11)	34
Sam Wills (10)	35
Tanya Lawson (11)	35
Kelly Duggan (11)	35
Rachael Painter (11)	36
Georgia Williams (10)	36
Elizabeth Kitson (10)	37
Sam Brown (10)	37
Tom Grimstead (11)	38
Ellie Loweth (9)	38
Bethan Taylor (9)	39
Cheyenne Jayne-Manning (9)	39
Jackson Bardsley (11)	40
Evie Davenport (7)	40
Abbie O'Sullivan (10)	41
Shorna Devney (8)	41
Jordan Wetter (11)	42
Jusef Behit (8)	42
Matthew Thorpe (11)	43
Chloe Johnsey (9)	43
Emily Edwards (11)	44
Joshua Bolton (10)	45
Adam Seddon (11)	46
Ryan Parry (11)	46
Matthew Watts (11)	47
Sophie Jones-Orchard (8)	47

Elm Tree House School, Cardiff

Linnéa Freear (10)	69
Yasmin Wright (9)	70
Alysha Leach-Nnadi (8)	70
Isabella MacGregor (9)	71
Hazen Noell (9)	71
Emily Howell (10)	72
Sophie Kosinski (10)	72
Robi Fulgoni (9)	73
Becky Green (9)	73
Holly Bickerton (11)	74
Ann-Kathrin Klein (9)	74
Olivia Jarvis (9)	75
Rose Lubin (10)	75
Elisabeth Lubin (10)	76
Caroline Lakin (10)	76
Georgina Collins (10)	77

Hendredenny Park Primary School, Caerphilly
Harrie Clemens (8)	77
Molly Allen (11)	78
Julia Williams (11)	78
Sam Adamson (10)	79
Rhydian Knox (11)	79
Elizabeth New (9)	80
Charlotte Cavill (10)	80
Bethan Pugh (10)	81
Saffron Lloyd (8)	81
Tirion Stevens (8)	82
Alys Lloyd (10)	82
Laura Bonar (10)	83
Rhian Knox (8)	84

Pantysgallog Primary School, Dowlais
Melissa Palmer (9)	84
Robyn Smith (9)	85
Courtney Barrett (10)	85
Lucy Evans (10)	85
Jonathan Powell (10)	86
Rebecca Kinsey (9)	86
Abby Evans (9)	86
Julia Astley (10)	86

Stacey Elliott (10)	87
Jordan Cleaver (10)	87
Kyron Sinnett (10)	87
Lauren Osborne (10)	87
Tyrion Jones (10)	88
Daniel Lewis (10)	88
Charlotte Johnson (9)	88
Kirsty Jones (10)	89
Gavin Llewellyn (10)	89
Catrin Owen (10)	89
Jessica Jones (10)	90

Pembroke Primary School, Bulwark

Alice Cooksey (9)	90
Megan Kelly (8)	91
Sian Cresswell (9)	92
Keiran Jones (9)	93
Cody Frowen (9)	94
William Thomas (9)	95
Emma Skidmore (9)	96
Kayla Viljoen (9)	97
Hannah Polhill (9)	98
Robbie Fisher (9)	99
Gemma Hall (9)	100
Jack Bevan (9)	101

Pendoylan CW Primary School, Cowbridge

Freddie Jones (11)	102
Matthew Popham (11)	102
Megan Phillips (11)	103
Millicent Jenkins (11)	103
Paisley Orchard-Brown (10)	104
Ella Sylvester (10)	104
Hannah Ballinger (11)	105
Ryan Hawkins (11)	105
Patrick O'Brien (10)	106
Jordan Guard (10)	106
Lowri Davies (10)	107
Clementine Haines (11)	107
Caitlin Sturgess-Webb (10)	108
Kentaro Abe-Donovan (10)	108

Thomas Orr (6)	125
Emma Popham (6)	125
Jonathan Mitchell (7)	126
Amelia Sylvester (6)	126
Alicia Archer (5)	126
Jade Riggs (10)	127
Louisa Knowles (6)	127
Megan Bradwick (5)	127
Taya Mouncher (11)	128
Sam Aston (5)	128
Ffion Smith (6)	128
James Wakely (11)	129
Alexander Lloyd (6)	129
Johanna Little (5)	129
Evie Amos (10)	130
Harry Horan (5)	130
Curtis Browning (6)	130
Molly Westlake (10)	131
Aniella Perrins (6)	131
Ellie Davies (5)	131
Charlotte Prichard (l8)	132
Thea Young (11)	132
Christopher Gray (8)	133
Imogen Humphreys (11)	133
Brittany Teague (11)	134
Peta Williams (8)	135
Jules Orchard-Brown (8)	136
Jacob Clutterbuck (11)	136
Nathaniel Cannon (7)	137
Daniel Peters (9)	137
Brogan Falshaw-Skelly (8)	138
Ruth David (8)	139
Kieran Moroney (8)	140
Pippa Loam (8)	140
James Little (8)	141
Danielle Murphy (9)	141
Ethan Hogg (8)	142
Lydia McCarthy (8)	142
Libby Mouncher (8)	143
Anwen Smith (8)	144
Oliver Bayer (7)	145
Lewis Morgan (8)	146

Michael Boon (8)   147
Aaron Parsons (8)   148
Oliver Lloyd (8)   148
Joshua Matthews (7)   149
James Williams (10)   149

Penybont Primary School, Bridgend
Kyle Reid (8)   150
Benjamin Cruickshank (8)   150
Hannah Evans (8)   151
Ryan Pickford (8)   151
Geraint Lang (8)   152
Luke Williams (10)   152
Jack Mantell (10)   152
Tyler Walsh (8)   153
Sam Townend (8)   153
Owen Smith (10)   153
Joshua James, Molly Powles, Jamie Smith, Imogen Stewart,
        Kirsty Bradley & Paisley Thompson-Bailey (9) 154
Heather Johnston (10)   154
Jamie-Leigh Morgan, Chelsee Davies, Lloyd Griffiths,
        Ashley Dobbs, Kate Evans & Lucy Richards (9)   155

Penyrenglyn Primary School, Treherbert
Jordan Louise Barclay (9)   155
Beth Moulsdale (9)   156
Hanna Wakeford (11)   156
Alexander Jenkins (9)   157
Nathan Williams (11)   157
Jordan Haskins (9)   158
Danielle Morgan (11)   158
Samantha Rees (9)   159
Laurie Edwards (10)   159
Michael Hill (9)   160

Radyr Primary School, Cardiff
Sophie Bird (8)   160
Olivia Kendall (10)   161
Lucy Fuszard (8)   161
Hannah Dykes (8)   162

Ben Hardie (8)	184
Robert Liguz (8)	184
Alex Brown (10)	185
Adam Morris (9)	185
Charlotte Smith (9)	186
Miriam Smith (8)	186
Katie Griffiths (10)	187
Daniel Perry (10)	187
Elliot Jones (10)	188
Gary Lee (10)	188
Joe Crossley-Lewis (8)	189
Hannah May Williams (8)	189
Briony Powell (9)	190
Susanna Smith (9)	190
Jack Hooper (9)	190
Taylor Sumers (9)	191
Isobel Eddy (7)	191
Rebecca Bunney (9)	191
Christina Berry (9)	192

St Therese's School, Port Talbot

Daniel Oglesby (9)	192
Leah Emery (8)	192
Travis Monks Landeg (8)	193
Hannah Piles (9)	193
Kalon Smithers (8)	193
Bethan Maund (9)	194
Carly Green (9)	194
Benjamin Jack Potts (8)	195
Emilie Potts (8)	195
Luke Ball (9)	196
Joshua Michael Ready (9)	196
Dominic Bamsey (9)	196
Jack Ormond Lewis (8)	197
Abigail May Jones (9)	197
Robert Morgan (9)	197

Tredegarville Primary School, Cardiff

Megan Williams (7)	198
Marie Chambers (9)	198
Shannon-Leigh Evans (8)	199

Atlanta Hewings (8)	199
Natasha Wilkinson (8)	200
Ross O'Connell (9)	200
Kyle Ellaway (9)	200

The Poems

My Very Own Kitten

I have my very own kitten,
It is as pretty as a rose,
It is as white as snow,
Its name is Snowy.

My kitten is as soft as a cushion,
Other kittens are big and small,
Some are stray, some are pets,
I have my very own kitten.

It is my job to look after her,
I feed her tuna,
She loves it,
I have my very own kitten.

I got her from the pet shop,
There was loads to choose from,
I picked her because she was the best,
I love her, she loves me.

Lauren House (9)
Bryn Hafod Primary School, Cardiff

My Bird

My bird's name is Spike,
He's got a spike on top of his head,
That's how he got his name.

He loves to fly on your head,
He loves to have his head scratched,
He likes to be picked up,
He likes seeds for his tea,
I love him, he loves me,
He's the best pet ever.

Lauren Holloway (9)
Bryn Hafod Primary School, Cardiff

My Little Pony

I have a little pony,
Skinny and bony,
She likes to eat her carrot,
While watching my parrot,
She wears a pretty bow,
All white like snow,
She wears pretty clips,
As yellow as chips,
She is as black as a mole,
In a dark, dark hole,
She likes to lay,
In a big bit of hay.

Hannah-Mae Chapman (9)
Bryn Hafod Primary School, Cardiff

My Little Kitten

I have a little kitten
And I call her Mitten,
She is as white as snow
And she wears a pretty pink bow,
She has the smallest softest paws,
But beware her sharp, sharp claws.

Emma Hill (9)
Bryn Hafod Primary School, Cardiff

The Cat And Me

I think I saw a 'putty' cat
Creeping up on me
I did, I did
Then he climbed up the tree
To see what he could see, see, see
And all that he could see, see, see, was me, me, me.

Ben Miles (9)
Bryn Hafod Primary School, Cardiff

Dodging Dolphins

I have a dolphin called Danny,
But he ain't really funny.
Though he's really soft,
I'd rather a pet bunny.

As I am splashing around,
Danny comes up to me.
It's really rather sad,
Because nobody's with me.

I feed him lots of tuna
Every single day,
I tried him with some honey,
But then he swam away.

When he came back,
I was very happy,
But then he had a poo,
So I put on his nappy.

I left him by the shore,
To see him later,
But when I came back,
He ordered from the waiter.

Dannielle Hunter (9)
Bryn Hafod Primary School, Cardiff

My Pet Rabbit

I have a pet rabbit,
Small and scruffy,
His fur is white as snow,
His tail is very fluffy.

I have a pet rabbit,
Kept in a cage,
He likes to play
And forces the door with rage.

Megan Adams (9)
Bryn Hafod Primary School, Cardiff

My Pet Dog

My little puppy small and scruffy,
I got him on my birthday.

My little puppy big and black,
He does everything with me.

My dog like a fish can swim very far,
I really enjoy his company.

My old dog in that coffin,
How could it happen to me?

Abigail O'Leary (9)
Bryn Hafod Primary School, Cardiff

My Funky Monkey

I have a funky monkey,
It is rather chunky,
It likes to dance,
You should see it prance,
It likes to play,
You should see it sway.

Paige King (9)
Bryn Hafod Primary School, Cardiff

My Pretty Little Kitty

I have a little kitty who is very pretty,
She likes to play in the snow,
I know that she is smart
And she plays
A special part
In my heart.

Emily Bartlett (9)
Bryn Hafod Primary School, Cardiff

I Have A Snail . . .

I have a snail, he leaves a trail
All over my garden wall
He is so wet and small
He leaves a trail all over my wall

His colour is red
His name is Fred
He has a big head
And he leaves a trail all over my wall.

Gabriella Bonifay (8)
Bryn Hafod Primary School, Cardiff

Grooving Pony

I am a pony that is skinny and bony
I like to sing
And dance along,
I groove every day,
In every way,
I'm a grooving pony.

Sophie Jones (9)
Bryn Hafod Primary School, Cardiff

My Baby Elephant

I've got a baby elephant
That is quite intelligent,
It can count up to ten,
So then I called it Ben,
I got it from India.

Rebecca Leadbeatter (9)
Bryn Hafod Primary School, Cardiff

I Had A Monkey That Was So Funky

I had a monkey, he was so bumpy
And he liked to be funky,
I had a monkey sitting on a tree
And he liked to be just like me.

Sinead Kuwale (9)
Bryn Hafod Primary School, Cardiff

Smelly Monkey

I had a monkey
And he liked to be bumpy
He was so scruffy and he smelt like cheese
And only on Monday he liked eating peas.

Samuel Griffin (9)
Bryn Hafod Primary School, Cardiff

An Everlasting Game

War is an everlasting game
Refereed by one man with his lethal army serving him,
Rugby is a two team game,
Refereed by one man with his allies on the sidelines,
Plus it only lasts for a bit longer than one hour,
War in rugby sometimes happens!
When one player tackles unfairly, the unruly one is sent off!
The war then ends!
War is a one man game!
Rugby is not!
Sport is fair!
War is not!

Tom Cole (10)
Clun Primary School, Neath

Black Sabbath

On the first day a Jew looked out of the train window,
He saw terror, pain and huge chimneys looking down at him like
vultures.

On the second day the Jew peered out of barbed wire,
He saw the sun, flowers and freedom,
He looked behind him, however and saw torture and captivity.

On the third day the Jew looked across at the children,
He saw fear and tears.

On the fourth day the Jew looked around him,
He saw killing, shooting, he saw a massacre.

On the fifth day the Jew looked up at the chimneys,
He saw smoke, he looked below and saw fire and heard screams.

On the sixth day the Jew looked into the soldier's eyes,
He saw rage and the Devil within,
He looked into the gun,
He saw black, he saw death!

On Black Sabbath, he saw harmony,
He saw no more killing,
He saw a land of white.

He saw peace!

Harri Morgan (11)
Clun Primary School, Neath

War

I am afraid of war like a fly is afraid of a spider!
War comes suddenly, like rain upon a rock,
I am afraid of war like a tree is afraid of autumn,
Like a baby is afraid of being taken away from its mother,
I am afraid of war like animals are afraid of sharks,
Like war, they too are swift, cunning, killing machines!

Owain Thomas (11)
Clun Primary School, Neath

Faces

Faces look at me as if I'm their mother,
Scared, terrified children looking out at me,
Their eyes are slit from starvation,
Their mouths are gasping from horror,
Faces of horror, pain and death.

Faces look at me as if I'm their father,
So innocent, from the look of their eyes,
Bones showing through their skin,
Faces of horror, pain and death.

Faces looking out at me, as if I'm their sister,
Horrified children stare out at me,
Starving to death through the wire,
Screaming is heard from behind the fence,
Faces of horror, pain and death.

Faces look out at me as if I'm their brother,
Their eyes glisten in the shining sun,
A baby is crying full of pain,
A voice is heard from Hitler's slaves.

Faces of horror, pain, death,
Faces look out at me as if I was family.

Laura Roberts (11)
Clun Primary School, Neath

War

I am afraid of war!
Like a tree is afraid of an elephant,
Like an elephant is afraid of a poacher,
Like a poacher is afraid of being caught!

I am afraid of war!
Like an evacuee is afraid of their new home!
Like a soldier is afraid to fight,
I am afraid of war!

Kieran Fry (11)
Clun Primary School, Neath

It All Goes Black!

The siren sounds,
I run, run for shelter,
I arrive, thinking about peace,
Why is my world at war?
Why does this have to happen?
When will it end?
Why did it begin?
What will happen to me?
A bomb becomes a stag racing towards me,
An enemy that wants me to die!
This shelter becomes a swan, protecting her young,
My heart is now racing, beating like a bass drum!
My emotions shattered by a bang!
Silence fills my head with nightmares.
An engine is heard,
Then click, click, click,
I know what this means!
Death has come to get me!
Then it all goes black!

Rory Gibson (11)
Clun Primary School, Neath

War

Blood, horror, death,
People screaming,
People dying,
Gunshots echoing all around me,
Houses surrounded with blazing fire,
Explosions filling the air,
Abandoned churches, collapsed buildings,
People evacuating the cities,
Others devastated,
Just staring at what little is left!

Gethin Kerrison (11)
Clun Primary School, Neath

Peace

Peace is a happy life!
It's friendliness between everyone!
Peace is being left alone to think of those who have died,
Peace is very happy because you can remember
Everything that has gone wrong
And how you put it right!
Peace has brilliant pictures that everybody enjoys,
It's so happy, I just can't describe it,
Peace is the best thing ever made in this world!

David Winter (9)
Clun Primary School, Neath

War

War is like thunder in the sky,
Like a sword going straight through you!
Like a nightmare you can't wake up from!
War is like a leopard ripping you apart,
Like a town being destroyed,
Like the world falling apart!
Like death travelling through the earth,
Not stopping!

Alex Morgan (11)
Clun Primary School, Neath

War

War is as sad as big raindrops falling from the sky,
War is as horrible as fire burning a city,
War is as loud as bombs dropping from the sky,
War is as lonely as a child who is lost,
War is as black as when I close my eyes,
War is like a tiger roaring through the jungle,
War is sad!

Kathryn Mainwaring (9)
Clun Primary School, Neath

This Is War!

War is black, cold and upsetting!
It smells like a burnt roast!
It feels like kindness has faded away!
Like heavy rain pouring down from the dark.
That is war!
The taste makes you feel sick,
Closing your eyes is scary!
It's like lightning has struck
And it's never going to go away,
War has never been this bad!

Zoe Morgan (10)
Clun Primary School, Neath

War

I am afraid of war,
Like a tree is afraid of autumn,
Like a human is afraid of death,
Like a bucket of water about to evaporate.
I am afraid of war,
Like the cat is afraid of a dog,
Like a mouse is afraid of a cat,
Like a flower is afraid of a shoe.

I am afraid of war!

Daniel Thomas (10)
Clun Primary School, Neath

Caring For Others

Why do we care?
Why do I care?
How many people in this world care about each other?
Some, but others, none!
Why can't everyone care about each other, not just themselves?
Why are some people so selfish?
As my teacher says, 'It costs nothing to be kind!'
Sadly, the selfish ones seem to think it does!

Chelcey Mock (10)
Clun Primary School, Neath

You!

You!
Your head is like a huge pumpkin,
You!
Your eyes are like small eggs.
You!
Your ears are like mini sprouts.
You!
Your nostril is like a mini orange.
You!
Your mouth is like a letter box.
You!
Your hands are like slimy snakes.
You!
Your belly is like a Smartie cookie.
You!
Your legs are like long sticks.
You!
Your backside is like Big Ben.

Elysia Stretton (9)
Cwrt-Yr-Ala Junior School, Cardiff

You!

You!
Your head is like a fat pumpkin.
You!
Your eyes are like shooting stars.
You!
Your nostril is like a giraffe's rough foot.
You!
Your mouth is like a long caterpillar.
You!
Your hands are like slimy spiders.
You!
Your body is like smelly pickles.
You!
Your legs are like plastic tubes.

Claire Spackman (9)
Cwrt-Yr-Ala Junior School, Cardiff

Cheetah

Though not a cheetah
I have spots
Though not a dog
I have four legs
Though not a cat
I have a tail
Though not a lion
I have sharp teeth
Wherever I go
I roar, roar, roar
What am I?
Leopard.

Ryan Dinapoli (9)
Cwrt-Yr-Ala Junior School, Cardiff

Stars So Bright

Stars shine so bright
Bright with a blazing glow
Glow in the sky
Sky so dark.

Dark as a cave, it's very spooky
Spooky in the night
Night so dark with shooting stars
Stars are twinkling very brightly.

Lauren Griffiths (9)
Cwrt-Yr-Ala Junior School, Cardiff

Amazing, Amusing Alliteration

Brilliant buzzing bee
Rough running rhino
Slithery slimy snake
Running rabbit
Creepy caterpillar.

Rhiannon Lewis (8)
Cwrt-Yr-Ala Junior School, Cardiff

School

Pens, rubbers and pencils we use,
But in maths we can get confused!
Welsh, science, history too,
These are the subjects we have to do,
Pens, rubbers and pencils we use!
So come and join us we're the
Cwrt-Yr-Ala crew!

Bethanne Evans (9)
Cwrt-Yr-Ala Junior School, Cardiff

Flowers

F resh as a cold glass of water
L itter affects their environment
O pen up your colourful petals
W ind blows the joy all around us
E ats the fresh soil which fills them
R efuse darkness, adores the sun
S urf the grass like a magical wave.

James Sell (10)
Cwrt-Yr-Ala Junior School, Cardiff

Running Out Of Light

The sun is like a jewel,
Up above our school,
It brightens up my day
And melts the class modelling clay,
What will we do without it?
What would we do without . . . ?

Jordan Dawson (10)
Cwrt-Yr-Ala Junior School, Cardiff

Amazing, Amusing Alliteration

Snapping slithering slimy snake
Rough running roaring rhino
Kung fu kangaroo
Punching prowling polar bear
Outrageous octopus
Dippy dopey donkey.

Jordan Day (8)
Cwrt-Yr-Ala Junior School, Cardiff

Holly Tree

H olly has lots of green spiky leaves
O ver and over baby holly grows
L ovely bright and green
L ighter and lighter as the leaves die down
Y ellow and crisp they fade away.

Joshua Weir (10)
Cwrt-Yr-Ala Junior School, Cardiff

In The Sea

Sparkling waves, dolphins diving,
Tropical fish, sharks biting
And fighting, fish gliding,
People swimming,
People playing in the sand,
Big sparkling sand on the island,
Pirate gold on the island,
No one has seen the island before.

Luke Wood (10)
Derwendeg Primary School, Hengoed

The Salty Sea

Lovely green palm trees swaying in the sun
Fish glowing in the ocean
Dolphins doing acrobatics in the salty sea
Sun burning like lava
Clear water like the junk has gone down a pipe
The water twinkling like stars.

Ieuan Elliot (9)
Derwendeg Primary School, Hengoed

The Magic Of Jamaica

Smooth dolphins jump through breaking waves,
Hermit crabs and rock pool fish swim through rocks,
Rugged seashells rest at the bottom of the deep blue sea,
Colourful scales on the slim fish swimming,
Peaceful islands full of adventure,
Pirate treasure, jewels, crowns, rubies and more!
Children on the beach making sandcastles,
Adults sunbathing under thatched parasols,
Golden sunrays ready to burn your skin,
Put on your suncream before it's too late,
Watch the speedboats whiz past spraying water,
Palm trees sway in the gentle breeze,
Slow-walking tortoises looking for the sea,
In Jamaica we have fun.

Sarah Fisher (10)
Derwendeg Primary School, Hengoed

The Caribbean Dream

Golden palm trees shaking in the breeze on a peaceful shore
Shining, swaying sea breaking in a sparkling sun
Delivering glimmering pirate gold
Darting dolphins gliding through the sea
Silver sun umbrellas sparkling in the shiny sun like ice cream cones.

Sasha Paget (10)
Derwendeg Primary School, Hengoed

Atlantic Beach

Glistening seashells washing on the sunkissed shore like tiny boats,
Dolphins gliding through the crystal ocean like sparkling arrows,
People strolling on the hot golden sand chatting happily,
Palm trees swaying in a warm breeze.

Sarah Greenslade (9)
Derwendeg Primary School, Hengoed

Jamaica Island

Smooth seashells on the sandy shore,
Colourful shells washed up by the crystal sea,
Sharp palm trees swishing in the breeze
Making it look like flying feathers,
Spiky starfish squirming in the glamorous sun
Like spiky glittering jewels,
Turtles lapping the waves having plenty of fun
Making all turtles join in the fun,
Swooping birds gliding about
Waiting for scaly fish to pop out,
Darting fish swimming around the big blue ocean,
Watching out for swooping birds,
Tiny crabs scuttling about pinching toes
With their tiny little pincers,
Plenty of people having fun in and out of the waves,
Sitting down on sunbeds getting a tan
In sunny, sunny Jamaica.

Ashlee Matthews (10)
Derwendeg Primary School, Hengoed

Starlight Burst

Ragged palm trees washed up by the gentle sea
Fish gliding through the restful ocean
Velvety sand so pure it's like you're looking in the mirror
Sun so hot it's like a ball of fire
Sky so blue it's like God's painted a perfect picture.

Kodie Mackay (9)
Derwendeg Primary School, Hengoed

Haiku

My bird is yellow
He is yellow with black stripes
Yellow as the sun.

Emily James (9)
Derwendeg Primary School, Hengoed

Magical Island

Cute rubber dolphins skim across the crystal blue ocean,
Tasty hot dog and burger stalls glide through the air,
Scaly, colourful fish dart and swish through the smooth turning sea,
Rough, small rocks that scratch on the rock pools,
A circular moat round a crooked old sandcastle,
The moat looks like a pool of potion,
People on the sinking gold sand,
Walking along the tide in bare feet,
Wooden parasols that block the fireball of sun
Like a meteorite coming to blow up the Earth.

Amy Baker (10)
Derwendeg Primary School, Hengoed

Sandy Shore

Golden sand on the shore
Golden seashells looking like pirate gold
Beautiful colourful rainbow fish darting through the sea
Little tiny shore fish enjoying themselves
Little children swimming like fish
Grown-ups sunbathing on the beach.

Matthew Jay (9)
Derwendeg Primary School, Hengoed

Fruit Bowl

The banana is a slide for the kids to slide down it,
The apple is a bouncy ball,
The bowl is a pond for the kids to look at,
The pear is a climbing frame,
The strawberry is a trampoline,
The cherry is a seat for the kids.

Paige Sanders (10)
Derwendeg Primary School, Hengoed

Summer Days

Swaying palm trees in the breeze like pretty fish swimming in the seas,
Colourful shells on legs climb to the rock pool hiding
                                    from the children,
Magical crystal dolphins race the boats flying on the top of the water,
Mums sunbathing in the yellow sun and dads getting buried
                                    in the sand by their kids.

A shark swims into the sea with the current, he licks his lips,
He dives under the water and eats a swarm of beautiful fish,
Everyone runs out of the sea and sits on the sand waiting for
                                    the shark to go away.

The shark has gone, everyone is back in the sea,
A cold breeze comes out of nowhere but people don't
                                    notice it's getting late.

Sadie Thomas (10)
Derwendeg Primary School, Hengoed

Haiku

I like my grandad
My grandad has got white hair
He rescued a cat.

Carly Osborne (9)
Derwendeg Primary School, Hengoed

Haiku

I like my mummy
She helps me with my homework
But she works a lot.

Amber Roberts (9)
Derwendeg Primary School, Hengoed

What's In Mr Jhon's Basement?

There are teachers eating spiders under a dusty trapdoor,
There's a slimy toad out for revenge,
A dragon breathing fire into the boiler of horror,
Demon bats swinging horridly,
Screaming rats running wildly,
A garden of fear,
Jingling keys you must obey,
Things lurk in the paint cans,
Terrifying tyres waiting for sports day,
Children eating the sweeping brush,
Spellbound footballs that break glass,
There's a Chinese python in there too!

That's what I think is in Mr Jhon's basement.

Jade Jones (9)
Derwendeg Primary School, Hengoed

Haiku

I've got a bracelet
It shines bright in the sunlight
It flashes with joy.

Sasha Kumar (9)
Derwendeg Primary School, Hengoed

Haiku

My dog likes football
He plays with us all the time
And likes scoring goals.

Rhys Spanswick (9)
Derwendeg Primary School, Hengoed

Alliteration

One orange octopus opening the little door
Two tanned tigers jumping up and down
Three tadpoles swimming in the deep water
Four frogs fishing for friends
Five flies flying in the air
Six seals slapping on the seashore
Seven spiders skating on the slide
Eight enormous elephants bathing on their tummy
Nine nasty newts nicking their newts
Ten tanned turtles tickling their tummy.

Abbi Parker (9)
Derwendeg Primary School, Hengoed

My Red Football Bag

My red football bag is a wrapped up stadium called Anfield,
My massive bag of marbles are the Liverpool fans,
My coloured pencils make the football goals,
My carpet sample is as green as the grass of the football field,
My mobile phone is the commentator's television monitor,
My library cards are the referee's offence indicator,
My cylindrical pencil case is the tunnel to the field,
My lunch box lid protects the football field from the rain.

Lewis Green (10)
Derwendeg Primary School, Hengoed

The Caribbean

Shining seashells glistening on the shore like measure,
Dolphins jumping up out of the sparkling ocean,
Crabs running over the warm golden shore,
Glowing starfish in the rock pools,
People sunbathing on the sparkling sand
A cool breeze rippling on the shore.

Nicole Fox (10)
Derwendeg Primary School, Hengoed

Our School

Our school, built in 1920,
Foreman bossing, wanting action,
Hammers banging silver nails,
Glass smashing, wood falling,
Cement splashing, bricks crashing,
Builders singing as they're drilling.

Our school, built in 1920,
Children laughing, teachers shouting,
Naughty boys getting into rows,
Girls singing, boys shouting,
Teachers talking very loud.

Shauna Day (10)
Derwendeg Primary School, Hengoed

My Class Table

My pot is the ship
My ruler is the plank that people walked
My pen is the flagpole
My pen top is the shark
The page is the land
The sharpener is a captain pirate
The colouring pencil is a cannon
My eraser is a flag.

Rhys Carroll (10)
Derwendeg Primary School, Hengoed

Haiku

I love my mother,
She helps me do my homework,
She is the best mum.

Ashley Dwyer (9)
Derwendeg Primary School, Hengoed

Alliteration

One orange ostrich opening a door,
Two turquoise turtles teaching a tiger,
Three tanned toads tickling a tadpole,
Four fawn foxes flicking lots of flies,
Five fluffy falcons flying with the frogs,
Six silver sharks skidding on the sea,
Seven scarlet snakes sliding down a slide,
Eight emerald elephants doing lots of exercise,
Nine nosy newts nosing at the needle,
Ten tangerine tigers trotting down to town.

Danial Huxter (9)
Derwendeg Primary School, Hengoed

Alliteration

One orange otter flicking the oak tree,
Two tangerine tigers tripping over toadstools,
Three turquoise tarantulas trotting to town,
Four fawn foxes finding fat fish,
Five funny falcons frightening frogs,
Six slimy snakes slithering down the slide,
Seven scarlet spiders singing a song,
Eight emerald eels electrocuting themselves,
Nine navy nutty newts cracking nutty nuts,
Ten tanned toads squishing tiny turtles.

Katie Aldridge (9)
Derwendeg Primary School, Hengoed

Haiku

One bright summer's day
The sun shone very brightly
Until it got dark.

Joe Williams (9)
Derwendeg Primary School, Hengoed

Christmas Poem

If there were no Christmas
I would miss
The wrapping paper flying about on the floor
The smell of the food on the table
The sound of the bells on the Christmas tape
The sight of children going round people's houses singing carols
And the children going down my street on sledges
It would be terrible not to have them again
The sparkling decorations on the wall
The rustling of the trees when the children get their presents
The feeling you get when you go downstairs and open your presents
It would be terrible without Christmas.

Lauren Dickens (9)
Derwendeg Primary School, Hengoed

Christmas Poem

If there were no Christmas
I would miss the Christmas crackers and the presents
The sound of Christmas bells and the Christmas carols
The sight of presents and the Christmas dinner
It would be terrible not to have them again
The Christmas tree and the sparkling snow
The feeling I get when I open my presents and the Christmas lights
It would be terrible without Christmas.

Lauren Emmett (9)
Derwendeg Primary School, Hengoed

Haiku

My dog's hair is brown
Her face is like a leopard
His name is Lenny.

Chelsea Hayes (9)
Derwendeg Primary School, Hengoed

Christmas Poem

If there were no Christmas
I would miss
The presents and singing
The sound of bells and reindeers
The sight of stockings and happy faces
And the scattered snow
It would be terrible not to have them again
The sparkling snow
The feeling you get
When I hear the sound of
Rustling of wrapping paper
It would be terrible without Christmas.

Tabitha Hughes (9)
Derwendeg Primary School, Hengoed

Alliteration

One orange octopus sitting on the water,
Two tanned tadpoles tripping over a tree,
Three tangerine tigers sitting on the floor,
Four fawn foxes singing on the sofa,
Five fawn frogs spinning in the sky,
Six silver spiders sitting on the bed,
Seven scarlet seals as little as can be,
Eight elephants sitting on an egg,
Nine navy newts swimming in the water,
Ten tiny turtles tripping to the town.

Belinda Nelmes (9)
Derwendeg Primary School, Hengoed

Haiku

My dog has black eyes
That sparkle in the night sky
And looks like mirrors.

Lucy Burke (9)
Derwendeg Primary School, Hengoed

Haiku

The sun rose slowly
In the greatest light blue sky
And back down again.

Geraint Dallimore (9)
Derwendeg Primary School, Hengoed

Haiku

My dog's hair is brown
His face is like a tiger
His name is Toffee.

Jack Wood (9)
Derwendeg Primary School, Hengoed

Mother's Day

You're a little drop of water
I catch you in my hands
I hold you tight
I make you warm
And then you transform into
The
Greatest
Mum
In the world
You read the news every day
And then you stop to have a play
But one thing I really do mind
Is that you keep on asking me the time
I love you
And
You love me
This is because
We're family.

Zoey Mitchell (10)
Durham Road Junior School, Newport

Enemy Attack

Out of the placid evening sky, the planes came screeching down,
Machine guns rattled as streams of bullets were fired at the town.
Like flying death they approach the murderous cries and groans
And people shiver, despite the cracking fire and the warmth
                                    of their houses and homes,
Others hear footsteps running in panic, trying desperately
                                    to escape the sound,
Too late! The whine and the thump of the bombs can be
                                    heard crashing to the ground
And the silences given you hear beating of the heart
And the wails of family whose fathers must depart,
As the darkness skulks away, the devastation is revealed
And the injured are rushed to hospitals where they will
                                    soon be healed.
As for the rest? Their grieving prayers pray for peace,
As they troop home they question, 'When will this cease?'

Ayesha Behit (10)
Durham Road Junior School, Newport

What Is Red . . .

The Queen's cloak, shiny and long,
My school tie silky and soft,
Hot strawberries dripping with juice,
One round cherry, soft and squishy,
My heart beating like mad after running round the playground,
Prefect badges shiny and hard,
Freshly picked roses from the florist,
My rosy cheeks after laughing,
Sunset, lovely and bright with lots of colours,
The post van with its logo, sometimes dirty,
Jam, sticky and yummy,
Our dragon standing proudly on our Welsh flag,
Blood squirting from my knee.

Kaidie-Jae Prytherch (8)
Durham Road Junior School, Newport

My Spell

As I walk around the cauldron,
I make something nice for children,
Mouldy chocolate I put in,
Which I found in the black bin.

Vegetable, vegetable make the cauldron bubble,
If you don't there'll be lots of trouble!

Sugar, yoghurt all mixed in,
That has come out of a silver tin,
Melting chocolate is so yummy,
I just can't wait when it's in my tummy.

Vegetable, vegetable make the cauldron bubble,
If not there'll be lots of trouble!

Now that I have finished, it's not so bubbly,
But I must say it looks so lovely,
All it needs is a bit of ice,
Now I'll have to feed it to the hairy mice.

Vegetable, vegetable make the cauldron bubble,
If not there'll be lots of trouble!

Rukhsar Hanif (11)
Durham Road Junior School, Newport

Air Raid

Collapsing buildings trapping people inside,
Crackling orange flames filling the war shattered city,
No hope for the future,
Wailing people begging for peace,
Then screaming as they realise their worst nightmares have come true,
Clouds of black smoke fill the air,
Bridges collapsing as people run trying to avoid the tumbling mess,
Screaming mothers crying for their children, hoping this is all a dream.
Air raid.

Chloe Pickering (10)
Durham Road Junior School, Newport

Moon Poem

The full moon shimmers
Like a mirror reflecting down to Earth,
The full moon
Is like a tin lid shining down on us.

Glowing bright in the night,
Disappearing when it's light.

The crescent moon glistens,
Like a cradle rocking a baby,
The crescent moon
Is like a yellow banana peeled.

Glowing bright in the night,
Disappearing when it's light.

The changing moon shrinks
Like a wet tissue absorbing water,
The changing moon
Is like a mouth opening and closing.

Glowing bright in the night,
Disappearing when it's light.

George McDonagh (8)
Durham Road Junior School, Newport

Air Raid

Just like in the movies war was declared.
Planes came screeching down over rooftops,
Dropping bombs as windows shattered into sprays of
                                        murderous fragments,
Screams of terror came to everyone's lips as planes came
                                        closer and closer,
Machine guns rattled as families protected their children,
Nazis ripped up the road like tearing the backbone from a fish.

Carmen Goodyear (9)
Durham Road Junior School, Newport

Moon Poem

The full moon glistens
Like a ten pence piece
The full moon
Is like a tennis ball

Glowing bright in the night
Disappearing when it's light

The crescent moon shines
Like a yellow banana
The crescent moon
Is like a bouncing boomerang

Glowing bright in the night
Disappearing when it's light

The changing moon shrinks
Like a popped balloon
The charging moon
Is like a white Malteser

Glowing bright in the night
Disappearing when it's light.

Curtis Jones (8)
Durham Road Junior School, Newport

The Sun Is . . .

The sun is . . .
A fiery Fanta ball in the desert
A friendly smiling face in the sky
A roaming lion in the sand
A spitting volcano spitting lava into the sky
A machine gun shooting down Meschersmitts
An M8 tranquillising the planes
A shotgun slaying crowds
The sun is a gun.

Daniel Buttigieg & Jake Sicolo (10)
Durham Road Junior School, Newport

Sea Haikus

Crab
Ruby coloured crabs
Scattered over the soft sand
By the pink sunset

Dolphin
Dipping through the sea
Diving through the crashing waves
Jumping in the air

Octopus
Slimy tentacles
His legs wriggle through the sea
He shines like jewels

Seagull
Seeking for its prey
He swoops down to catch his food
Now it's time to eat.

Sheridan Lacey (11)
Durham Road Junior School, Newport

Tiger, Tiger

Tiger, tiger
Body sleek and sly
Pouncing on prey
Hunting all day

Tiger, tiger
Gleaming golden eyes
Looking for prey
Eating all day

Tiger, tiger
Swimming with style
Hiding from prey
Soaking all day.

Declan Henry (9)
Durham Road Junior School, Newport

Moon Poem

The full moon rolls
Like a shiny diamond
The full moon
Is like a glimmering basketball

Glowing bright in the night
Such a sight from a height

The crescent moon rocks side to side
Like a juicy banana
The crescent moon
Is like a glimmering star

Glowing bright in the night
Such a sight from a height

The changing moon fades away
Like a squashed ball
The changing moon
Is like a thin piece of string

Glowing bright in the night
Such a sight from a height.

Alice Sayle (9)
Durham Road Junior School, Newport

Sea Haikus

Sailing in the sea
Dolphins splashing everywhere
Swimming gracefully

Sea horses swimming
Away from the scary sharks
Everyone happy

People all around
Deckchairs on the golden sand
Seashells everywhere.

Jessica Moore (11)
Durham Road Junior School, Newport

Troll Began

Troll began
He took the tusks of an elephant
He stole the sharpness of rats' claws
And made his teeth

For his arms
He took the muscles from the world's strongest man
He robbed the strength of a stone
He stole the mane of a horse

From the ocean
He took the clashing of the waves
He stole the jaggedness of a cliff
For his thundering voice

Then he took the shape of the Earth
Troll robbed the shadow of the moon in the night sky
He took a pinch of golden sand
To make his luminous eyes
And troll was made.

Hollie Kehoe (11)
Durham Road Junior School, Newport

Summer

Sun reflecting down
Children splashing everywhere
Parents with sunburn.

Chelsea Powell
Durham Road Junior School, Newport

The Sea

The blue crystal sea
Is crashing against the rock,
The gigantic waves.

Ryan Perkin (11)
Durham Road Junior School, Newport

Troll Began

Troll began,
He took the thunder from the storm,
He took the beating of the waves
And made his booming voice.

For his strong muscles,
He took the strength of rocks,
He took the shape of a full moon,
He took the size of a vast boulder.

From the terrifying shark,
He grabbed the jagged razor teeth,
He snatched the powerful jaws
For his gigantic mouth.

Then stole the sharpness of the sword,
Troll captured the pointed teeth of a giant lion,
He pinched the sparkle from hard steel,
To make his sharp claws
And troll was made.

Sam Wills (10)
Durham Road Junior School, Newport

Seashells Haiku

White seashells scattered,
Sprinkled over golden sand,
Seashells sunbathing.

Tanya Lawson (11)
Durham Road Junior School, Newport

The Night Sea Haiku

Stars glistening down
Reflecting on soft waters
Calmly still, for now.

Kelly Duggan (11)
Durham Road Junior School, Newport

To Turn Ben's Hair Green

Round and round the cauldron goes,
Mixed with some frogs' toes,
Gruesome mould from my bread,
This is a meal which some witches are fed.

Buckets of green horrible slime,
Ben's hair is going to be lime.

In I clunk the eyes of a newt,
Even with some gone off fruit.
The cauldron is starting to bubble,
There is going to be some trouble.

Buckets of green horrible slime,
Ben's hair is going to be lime.

Snakes are going in next,
This potion is the best,
It is finally starting to smell,
Now it's time to cast the spell.

Buckets of green horrible slime,
Ben's hair is finally lime.

Rachael Painter (11)
Durham Road Junior School, Newport

Isabel

Isabel, Isabel met a snake
Isabel, Isabel felt her hand shake
The snake was hungry, the snake was bad
The snake's mouth was jagged, tough and hard
The snake said, 'Isabel glad to meet you'
'How do Isabel, now I'll eat you!'
Isabel, Isabel wasn't worried
Isabel, Isabel didn't scream or scurry
She rolled her curls and she washed her hands
Then Isabel ate him and spat his bones in the sand.

Georgia Williams (10)
Durham Road Junior School, Newport

Sealife Haikus

The sea
The rough washing waves
Crashing against the grey rocks
Shimmering blue sea

The whale
The slimy wet whale
Swimming through the foamy sea
Scaring fish away

The noise
The noisy dolphins
As loud as a laughing clown
The boats beep their horns

The colour
The crystal blue sea
The shiny fishes swimming
The lush green seaweed.

Elizabeth Kitson (10)
Durham Road Junior School, Newport

The Sun Is . . .

The sun is . . .
A hot fiery spitting volcano
A golden sandy desert
A tangy bottle of Fanta
A flaming ball of heat
A golden blanket covered with sweetness
A single shadow not to be seen
A roaring lion ready to pounce
A swirling sunflower
A yellow friendly smiling face
A place where dreams come from
Hot
Fiery
Desert!

Sam Brown (10)
Durham Road Junior School, Newport

Haikus

Crab
The crab trails the beach
Chasing after its new prey
For luscious new food

Sea
The dark deep blue sea
Crashing up against the boat
Killing the fishes

Dolphins
Dolphins move swiftly
Moving through the blue ocean
Calling for their young

Seagull
Seeking for its prey
Swooping down to catch fishes
Looking for its egg.

Tom Grimstead (11)
Durham Road Junior School, Newport

Snowman Melting

Snowman melting
In the sun
He has always
Had fun
Today is his last
No snow games
No scarf to keep him warm
No stones to keep him smiling
Winter sun warming through
Snowman no more
See you next winter
Mr Snowman.

Ellie Loweth (9)
Durham Road Junior School, Newport

Four Seasons Dragon

Dragon of spring sees new flowers and trees,
She is as pink as a primrose,
She is in the garden planting,
She is jumping and playing with her friends,
The spring dragon sees new flowers and trees.

Dragon of summer sees a big golden sun,
He is golden and silver, he glitters!
He is posing on the beach,
He is licking an ice cream,
The dragon of summer sees a big golden sun.

Dragon of autumn smells crispy leaves,
She is crispy brown,
She jumps in the leaves gracefully,
Her teeth chatter as she lands,
The autumn dragon smells crispy leaves.

Dragon of winter smells nothing but ice,
He is a bluebell blue and his nose is pointed,
His legs are moving rapidly,
He is turning curiously,
Stomping fiercely along the icy snow,
The winter dragon smells nothing but ice.

Bethan Taylor (9)
Durham Road Junior School, Newport

The Sea

The sea is a swooping eagle,
The waves are its jagged claws, feathers and sharp beak,
Splashing the pointed rocks as if its flying fast,
The 'eagle' dives for fish,
The turbulence crashing down.
When it swoops back up the birds of the air feed their families,
It's as if the sea is forming a tidal wave,
His sharp eyesight makes him quick and clever.

Cheyenne Jayne-Manning (9)
Durham Road Junior School, Newport

My Seasonal Garden

The spring garden is emerald-green
The lime colour grass in the garden
Little lambs being born, taking their first steps
The sun glistening on the ground

The summer garden is the season of fire
People burning with sunbathing
The sun as real as a rose
Children dive into the vast ocean to keep themselves cool

Flowerbeds swaying with colour
The autumn garden is brown and dark
As you walk through your garden leaves crackle under your feet
The brown and golden leaves falling off the trees
Where's the colour gone?

The winter garden is as white as snow
Children making snowmen in the garden
No one able to get to work because of the snow
Paw prints in the glistening ground
Winter has definitely taken over.

Jackson Bardsley (11)
Durham Road Junior School, Newport

Red Is . . .

Tomato ketchup drizzling from its bottle,
My heart pumping because I have run a mile,
Cherries tasting sweet as I pop them in my mouth,
A squirrel with shining fur,
Lots of children wearing prefects' badges,
A dangerous fire in the house,
Lots of blood in my body,
The glistening new roses from my sweetheart,
The gorgeous sunset rising up,
My shiny lips which help me to talk,
The Royal Mail post van which drives and delivers the mail.

Evie Davenport (7)
Durham Road Junior School, Newport

The Writer Of This Poem

(Based on 'The Writer of this Poem' by Roger McGough)

The writer of this poem
Is as jiggy as can be,
But my friends think I am so funny,
All the boys just love looking at me.

As nice as an angel,
As groovy as a hippy,
As popular as a film star
And I like a lot of lippy.

As smooth as a slippery floor,
As slow as a snail,
As small as a chimpanzee,
As majestic as a whale.

The writer of this poem
Is surely number one,
She's on the top of the world,
Look at me everyone!

Abbie O'Sullivan (10)
Durham Road Junior School, Newport

What Is Red?

Red is . . .
A Royal Mail post van
Driving through the town.
My blood pumping in my body.
The post box full up with letters.
A raspberry in my tummy.
My tomato sauce splatting on my plate.
I see some fire up the hill.
That squirrel in the tree.
Roses growing on a bush.
My lips shining on me.
Heat as warm as can be.
A tomato with seeds inside.

Shorna Devney (8)
Durham Road Junior School, Newport

The Writer Of This Poem

(Based on 'The Writer of this Poem' by Roger McGough)

The writer of this poem
Is as tall as a tree
As funny as Mr Bean
As stunning as can be

As strong as a brick
As fast as a bee
As thin as a stick
As cheeky as a monkey

As handsome as a king
As nice as a flower
As strong as an ox
As strong as Superman's power

The writer of this poem
Is as sweet as apple pie
He owns his own mansion
But I think it's all a lie!

Jordan Wetter (11)
Durham Road Junior School, Newport

What Is Red?

Red is . . .
Fresh, lovely, watery cherries.
Thick, liquidy blood,
Big, oozy piles of tomato sauce,
My cheeks when it's cold,
The Royal Mail box,
Poppies bright and happy,
Jam sticky, cold, dark and tasty,
A squirrel big and fat,
Dragon light, strong and scaly,
Sunset beauty to a man's eye,
Cherry, juicy, watery and soft,
Watermelon soft, oval and with seeds inside.

Jusef Behit (8)
Durham Road Junior School, Newport

The Writer Of This Poem

(Based on 'The Writer of this Poem' by Roger McGough)

The writer of this poem
Is as small as a bee,
As stupid as Mr Bean,
Ask me to help, I say, 'What me?'

As strong as Superman,
As wrong as an X,
As sneaky as an ant,
I guess I'm like Becks.

As spotty as a leopard,
As funny as a clown,
As hot as Naples,
I won't give you a frown.

The writer of this poem
Is the biggest pop star,
He's probably the best
And hopes to go far!

Matthew Thorpe (11)
Durham Road Junior School, Newport

The Wave

The wave crashing into boats,
Bashing into rocks reaching for the mountains,
Smashing ships,
Sea monsters fighting with waves,
Crashing into people,
Jumping over sea creatures,
Meandering around and around,
Destroying boats,
Twirling around and up and down,
Stopping boats from sailing,
Going up to the sea,
Trapping sea animals.

Chloe Johnsey (9)
Durham Road Junior School, Newport

War On Mars

Stomp, stomp
The feet of the soldiers marching
The road to death had begun
Suddenly *bang* the first deadly bullet is shot
The war has started
There's no going back
One after another bullets are shot
Shattering hearts and houses
Blood staining helmets
People fishing in blood
Blood streaming from their arms and legs
Boom the biggest bomb so far
Children killed
Animals petrified
Only a few standing
'Let's kill them,' is heard

All is silent,
All has ended,
So they think!
Then *boom* goes a cannon
Bang goes a gun
All visible is destruction
A deathly silence occurs
All souls dead
War on Mars has ended
A graveyard is all that's left.

Emily Edwards (11)
Durham Road Junior School, Newport

A Spell To Create A Troll

A boom of thunder,
Dream of wonder,
In we throw cod liver oil,
A venomous snake's large round coil,
A tongue of a frog,
The gruesome slime from a bog.

Triple, triple, steam and sizzle,
Added with some gloomy drizzle.

Lungs of a gigantic bat,
The big fat tail of a squealing rat,
The rotting toenail of a child,
An eyebrow of a cat in the wild,
The tooth of a bloodthirsty vampire,
A magma ball from the fire.

Triple, triple, steam and sizzle,
Added with some gloomy drizzle.

A baboon's bottom,
An ancient mummy that is rotten,
Eyes of a silent owl,
Sound of a werewolf that howls,
Nostrils of a looming dragon,
Pace of a tumbling wagon.

Triple, triple, steam and sizzle,
Added with some gloomy drizzle.

Joshua Bolton (10)
Durham Road Junior School, Newport

A Spell To Make Something Double

Bubble, bubble make some trouble
Try to make something double!

First you add the head of a human drab,
The pierced eyes of a rotten crab,
Now drop in rough, golden hair,
Torn from the menacing grizzly bear!

Bubble, bubble make some trouble,
Try to make something double.

Secondly stir in the decapitated lobster tail,
Tear from the sea the ribcage of an angry killer whale,
Shortly after shove in one million biting gnats,
To end this spell add the bloodthirsty vampire bats.

Bubble, bubble make some trouble,
Try to make something double!

Adam Seddon (11)
Durham Road Junior School, Newport

Spell Poem

In the cauldron boil and bake
Sling in the twentieth fruity cake
Pelt in 40 ten pound notes
And fill the cauldron with extra goats

Once I get all the money
I will go and boil my mummy

In the cauldron boil and bake
The richest boy which is Jake
Let's go and boil another purse
But not the one from the lovely nurse

Once I get all the money in
I'm gonna boil my mummy.

Ryan Parry (11)
Durham Road Junior School, Newport

Today's Newport

Newport in the year 2004
Is nothing like it was before,
Lorries, cars and buses too,
Horse and carts are very few.

People busy everywhere,
Not much time to stand and stare.
Lots of bright, shiny lights,
Glowing through the darkest nights.

Aeroplanes droning up above,
Hard to hear a cooing dove.
Cars go past making lots of noise,
While children play with electronic toys.

Shops are selling plastic gifts,
People go upstairs in moving lifts.

The old castle still stands with its grassy moat,
Down in the muddy river still go the boats.

Matthew Watts (11)
Durham Road Junior School, Newport

Red Is . . .

Sweet, juicy apples hanging from an apple tree
A postbox standing full of glittery white letters
A car stopping at the shiny traffic light
Cheeks, rosy-red
Ketchup squirting all over your food
Your heart pumping blood around your body
Sunset just starting to rise behind the clouds
A terrific school tie, bright and shiny
The dragon stood blowing flames on the Welsh flag
A strawberry being picked off a tree
Roses with lovely shells of sweetness
A squirrel cracking open his nuts.

Sophie Jones-Orchard (8)
Durham Road Junior School, Newport

The Writer Of This Poem
(Based on 'The Writer of this Poem' by Roger McGough)

The writer of this poem
Is as tall as a tree,
As quiet as a mouse,
As sly as can be.

As cheeky as a monkey,
As silly as a clown,
I am so funky
And I never wear a frown.

As cool as a cucumber,
As quick as lightning,
As chatty as a parrot
And not very frightening.

The writer of this poem
Never ceases to amaze,
She's number one
Or so she says.

Katie Porter (11)
Durham Road Junior School, Newport

Rocket Ride

R umbling, rolling, rocket racing to the sky,
O rbiting over orange lights,
C reaking, crumbling, crashing closer,
K nuckles as white as ice cream,
E lectrifying ending, exploding engines,
T erminating, twisting, tossing tummies.

R ushing, reaching, rattling roar,
I ll but enjoying ice cream,
D ipping down to safety,
E ager, tripping to get off.

Christopher Veary (9)
Durham Road Junior School, Newport

A Spell To Make A Football Player

Michael Owen's pace
Steven Gerrard's grace

In my pot I will add a Liverpool shirt
From the pitch pour some grass and dirt
Sprinkle in some football boots
To give him a powerful shoot

Michael Owen's pace
Steven Gerrard's grace

Stir in some injury time
To make these spells seem simply fine
Throw in some angry fans
As they jump about in the stands

Michael Owen's pace
Steven Gerrard's grace

Finally add the Premiership cup
I want to hold it up
Mix in the Premiership teams
How well my spell seems.

Ben Woodward (11)
Durham Road Junior School, Newport

The Rocket Ride

R ocket rumbles up to the scary sky,
O n up to the black sky,
C rying children, scared,
K nuckles white as white,
E cho through the night,
T errified children screaming and crying.

R iding slowly going down,
I mpossible to enjoy,
D anger coming to an end,
E verybody eager to get off!

Benjamin Dorling (9)
Durham Road Junior School, Newport

Troll Began

Troll began
He snatched the stiffness of a cage
He grasped the roughness of a tree
For his bones

For his heart
He grabbed the smallness of an insect
He grasped the hatefulness of a snake
He pinched the harness of a bone

From a cave
He took the sharpness of an icicle
He stole the roundness of a moon crescent
For his teeth

Then at evening
He nabbed the redness of blood
He snatched the sharpness of an eagle
For his eyes

Swampland and sludge
Went into the smell of his breath
And for its fog
He caught the darkness of smoke
And Troll was made.

Alexander Adams (11)
Durham Road Junior School, Newport

My Seasonal Garden

The spring garden is as green as the new leaves on a tree,
The daffodils are as yellow as a banana,
The baby lambs are being born,
Their coats are as white as snow,
The spring garden is a beautiful place to be.

The summer garden is as red as a cherry,
The boiling hot air hits your face,
People wearing just T-shirts and shorts.

Samantha Hughes (11)
Durham Road Junior School, Newport

Troll Began

Troll began
He seized the roughness of the stones
He borrowed the shape of the trees
And made his bones

To make the smell of his breath
He caught the odour of rotten eggs
He stole the scent of the frog
And his breath was made

For his nose
He snatched the shape of the mountains
He stole two hollow caves
And his nose was made

His teeth needed
The blackness of the night
The sharpness of glass
And the shape of bricks

And Troll was made!

Samantha Mazey (10)
Durham Road Junior School, Newport

What Is Red?

Red is . . .
A rose as sweet as your lips,
A tomato as colourful as a rose,
A sign redder than lips,
My cherry is round and juicy,
The dragon is standing proudly on his flag,
My blood is redder than lips,
Your lips are sweeter than raspberries.

Joseph O'Flaherty (8)
Durham Road Junior School, Newport

Newport Today

I was walking through Newport City yesterday,
The shops were too busy for me to stay,
I went past the clock and I saw litter,
This made me feel very bitter,
I could see footballs, tennis and even rugby balls,
But then I saw graffiti that covered the walls,
Later on I ate fish and chips,
Indeed it made me lick my lips,
I heard police sirens ringing,
I also heard the choir singing,
There were plenty of roundabouts and car parks,
I could see lots of landmarks,
I was walking past my home street,
Yes, this day was a special treat.

Gavin Ruffell (11)
Durham Road Junior School, Newport

What Is Red?

Red is . . .
A raspberry sweet, nice and delicious,
The watermelon flesh,
A juicy plum that is yummy,
Strawberry juice trickling down on the floor,
Your blood,
A school tie,
The traffic light for stop!
Jam, so nice,
The dragon standing proudly on the Welsh flag,
Our lips which help us talk,
My cheeks as I blush,
A danger sign.

Lewis Slocombe (7)
Durham Road Junior School, Newport

I Wonder If I Can? . . . No, I Don't Think So!

A white root can burrow
And find moisture,
But it can't sing
Or rhyme like a poet.

A tall stem can catch your eye
And climb the wall,
But it can't catch a cloud
Or fly like a bird.

The beautiful bud can roll like a ball
And burst out like a bomb,
But it can't hop like a frog
Or swim like a fish.

Jamie Gane (11)
Durham Road Junior School, Newport

What Is Red?

Red is . . .
The lovely fresh rose from a secret garden.
A round plum picked from the tree.
My heart pumping every second.
The squirrel jumping high into the air.
Watermelon flesh so sweet and sometimes sour.
That raspberry jam, nice and bright.
The sunset rising over the yellow sun.
Our Welsh dragon breathing so much fire.
Tomato ketchup, so horrible, I don't like it!
My lips which help me to say my manners,
The warning signs that help my daddy to slow when men work.
The traffic light that helps my mummy to drive.
A poppy, the flower that will remind us about the war.

Lois Aspinall (8)
Durham Road Junior School, Newport

What Is Red?

Red is . . .
The sunset, lovely and colourful makes everyone smile.
A sweet smell of a poppy.
My heart so neatly made.
My cheeks all bright when I blush.
I put sauce on my dinner and tea sometimes.
I saw a baby squirrel in the park.
I put lovely jam on my toast.
My school tie is a nice thing to wear.
My lips help me to talk and eat.
Lovely cherry tomato.
My blood so deep and painful.

Emily Fowler (7)
Durham Road Junior School, Newport

Red Is . . .

One big, shiny, juicy, sweet plum.
A small, clean, fresh cherry.
Big, fierce, scary, loud dragon.
The Queen's cloak smooth, soft and pretty.
A long, smooth tie you wear.
My ketchup, yummy, tasty.
Squirrels climbing big, brown trees.
A bright beautiful rose I give my mum.
Jam, tasty, wobbly and squashy.
My cheeks go boiling hot.
Raspberries are bumpy, juicy and yummy.
A shiny, metal prefect badge.

Corey Cosslett (8)
Durham Road Junior School, Newport

Mars

Armies approaching the battlefield,
Alien monsters approaching,
Men fighting, swords clashing, shields protecting,
More men gathering,
Arrows flying,
A giant monster approaching,
Men fighting the beast, but unsuccessful,
More and more men arriving,
The beast is down, struggling,
Struggling, finally the beast is up again,
More arrows fly,
Men dying, dying,
Eventually all of the men are dead,
The monster too weak to go on,
The beast falls dead,
A ball of lightning,
Suddenly a bolt of lighting
Strikes the beast,
He is reduced to a pile of ashes,
All that's left is bodies, blood and ashes.

Ieuan Farley (11)
Durham Road Junior School, Newport

What Is Red?

Red is . . .
The sweet smell of a rose,
A freshly-picked poppy,
My big juicy plum I bought today,
The Queen's cloak sparkling with glitter,
A newly-picked strawberry smelling sweet,
My big raspberry I picked today,
The burning smell of fire.

Sophie Challenger (7)
Durham Road Junior School, Newport

A Spell To Make It Summer All Year Round

Summer, summer all year round,
There'll be forest fires on the ground.

First I'll put in suntan lotion,
To get one step further to concocting my potion.
Stirring in a sunbed,
Hoping not to get too burnt and red.

Summer, summer all year round,
There'll be forest fires on the ground.

Colours of orange and yellow,
Lying in the sun feeling mellow.
Add in some chocolate ice cream,
I hope I don't get sunburnt, cos I'll scream.

Summer, summer all year round,
There'll be fires on the ground.

In I throw a cooling fan,
The sun will give the world a tan.
Next sprinkle in sunglasses
And the beach population will rise in masses.

Summer, summer all year round,
There'll be forest fires on the ground.

Last I put in a swimming pool
And quickly you'll be really cool.
Toss in lots of shade,
Before the sun begins to fade.

Summer, summer all year round,
There'll be forest fires on the ground.

Harley Ault (11)
Durham Road Junior School, Newport

A Spell To Have A House Made Out Of Junk Food

In the boiling pot I place,
A large liquorice lace.

A stick of rock,
A chocolate lock.
A carton of chips,
Some strawberry lips,
A load of rainbow drops,
A box of lollipops.

In the boiling pot I place,
A large liquorice lace.

A large cake,
A crumbling flake,
A bottle of Sprite,
A Turkish delight,
A bowl of ice cream,
A small bar of Dream.

In the boiling pot I place,
A large liquorice lace.

A Christmas chocolate log,
A skinny hot dog,
A candy cane,
A greedy stomach pain,
Now my potion is complete,
I will be in for a massive treat.

In the boiling pot I place,
A large liquorice lace.

Laura Ryan (11)
Durham Road Junior School, Newport

A Spell To Make A Giant Monkey

Animal trouble, bubble, bubble
Now the monkey's size will double!

Gather around the boiling pot
All the wicked ingredients, there are a lot!
The hairy armpits of a monkey, the tiny brains of a dog
The bulging eyes of a bull, the smelly sweat of a hog!

Animal trouble, bubble, bubble
Now the monkey's size will double!

The essence of gruesome slug slime,
The hooves of a darkened menacing horse!
Then we throw in some of Hell's fiery
Blazing force!

Animal trouble, bubble, bubble
Now the monkey's size will double!

Then in goes the thick, poisonous venom
Of a deadly rattlesnake!
Then this evil, devilsome and mysterious broth
Will bubble and bake!

Animal trouble, bubble, bubble,
Now the monkey's size will double!

The blood of a human from a freshly-cut wound,
A vicious crocodile's slimy scale!
The battered bones of a great white shark,
The slippery, disgusting blubber of a killer whale!

Animal trouble, bubble, bubble
Now the monkey's size will double!

Now the mischievous concoction is finally done!
Let's find a wild and outgoing monkey
And have some tremendous fun!

Animal trouble, bubble, bubble,
Now the monkey's size will double!

Tobias Robertson (10) & Joshua Cranton (11)
Durham Road Junior School, Newport

Troll Began

Troll began
He stole the wind for his heavy breath
He captured the grumble of the trapped souls for his voice
He grabbed the roar of the lion for his shout
Then his voice was complete

Troll abducted rotten bones from graves
For his teeth and sharpened them with a blood-soaked sword
He nabbed the skin of the warty soggy toad for his tongue
From the leathery skin of the snake he made his lips
His mouth was complete

His skin was made from rough tree bark
His hair was from the branches
From the slimy frogspawn
He made his eyes
But there was one thing that wasn't finished
That was his skin
He hijacked the slime from the most slimy swamp
And added some vomit for the finishing touch
And then his skin was complete

The troll made his weapon from the stone of mountains,
He stole the horn of the rhino for spikes
His weapon was complete

He searched for his stomp
He captured the boom from Hell
He snatched the rumble from the earthquake
And his stomp was complete

He kidnapped the anger from the volcano for his temper
And the redness from the human blood
His fury was complete

From the coldness of the North Pole
And the hardness of a diamond
He made his heart

Troll was made.

Paige Dando (11)
Durham Road Junior School, Newport

I Wonder If It Can? . . . No, I Don't Think So!

The roots can grow in the earth
And search for moisture in the ground,
But they can't fly as gracefully as a bird,
Or jump as high as a kangaroo.

A stem can grow as tall as a house
And watch his fellow friends grow,
But it can't swim like a fish in the sea,
Or run as fast as a cheetah.

The pollen can allow the bees to eat
And stick to an insect's leg,
But it can't sit on a wooden seat,
Or weep as much as a cloud.

Conor Betts (11)
Durham Road Junior School, Newport

Mars

Two aggressive armies emerge from nowhere
Swords slash, armies battle
Without giving up on Mars, bringer of war!
Terrified children run as thunder booms overhead!

Gladiators battle on bloodstained Mars
Swords pierce into hearts on Mars, bringer of war!
Boom the beast appears out of the clouds on bloodshed Mars
He fights though, outnumbered, he swishes his sword endlessly

The mighty beast crashes
Surrounded in blood and soldiers
Finally the war is over . . .

Alexander Griffiths (11)
Durham Road Junior School, Newport

The Writer Of This Poem

(Based on 'The Writer of this Poem' by Roger McGough)

The writer of this poem
Is as sweet as honey,
As jazzy as a singer,
I have lots of money.

As shiny as stars,
That's what I can be,
As cheeky as a chimp,
As sparkly as the sea.

As twinkling as the moon,
As slow as a snail,
As graceful as a dancer,
As slimy as a whale.

The writer of this poem
I'm surely number one,
She's on top of the world,
Look out everyone.

Rhiannon Flage (11)
Durham Road Junior School, Newport

I Wonder If It Can? . . . No, I Don't Think So!

A colourful petal can quiver and shake
And catch my eye in the light,
But it can't climb up a fence,
Or run across the yard!

The emerald leaves can sway in the breeze
And give shade to the bright white roots,
But they can't sing and definitely can't dance
Or jump like a kangaroo!

The delicate flowers can smell like honey
And make the air very fresh,
But they can't swim like dolphins
Or fly in the air like a bird!

Natalie Abraham (11)
Durham Road Junior School, Newport

To Make Teachers Disappear

Double trouble on the way
Teachers, teachers, it's time to pay

First you add a dead sickening dog
Then add a poisonous dead frog
The head of a rattlesnake
To put in their big cake

Double trouble on the way
Teachers, teachers, it's time to pay

Last put in a disgusting eye
Then the leg from a venomous fly
Next a struggling newt
And take away the music from a flute

Double trouble on the way
Teachers, teachers, it's time to pay.

Cara Beech (10)
Durham Road Junior School, Newport

Newport Today

In Newport City the other day,
I heard the clock ticking away,
As I walked I saw some litter,
Which made me feel very bitter,
Then I heard a great big sound,
I'm walking past the rugby ground,
Later I go for something to eat,
I see lots of houses in the street,
As I peeped over the wall,
I saw a man with a rugby ball,
There's hardly any fields here,
With very little wildlife near,
All over the walls are graffiti,
That was my trip to Newport City.

Robyn Martin (11)
Durham Road Junior School, Newport

Snow

S now glistening in the sunrise
N ippy blizzards in the wintry mountains
O f all the seasons this is the best
W hite shimmering candyfloss from the winter fair spread
                                        over the fields

I n the streets young children collect the snow off cars and throw it
S ilvery blankets spread over the meadows

T he joy of winter is the bitter snow
H igh pine trees with candyfloss on the top
E ndless snowflakes falling

B itter coldness all around
E xcellent landscapes for artists to draw
S lippery ice on the ground and cars
T ipped sugar from the sky that's what snow is

Snow is the best!

Miriam Collett (10)
Durham Road Junior School, Newport

Rocket Ride

R ocket racing in the sky
O bserving people down below
C lutching the metal
K nuckles white as snow
E xcitedly screaming out loud
T errified feelings inside

R acing round and round
I mpatient to get off
D eafening screams
E ndless ride comes to an end.

Bobbi Cootes (9)
Durham Road Junior School, Newport

Legging The Tunnel

A very long pipe, but very thin,
Into the tunnel the boat goes in
The boat swims through, right by the wall
By shadowy figures very tall
Waves like hands, the boat goes through
Grim faces in the water, looking back at you

A man pushes his feet along the roof
While above you can hear the horses hooves
The shadows get bigger when you stretch out wide
While pushing the boat faster, builds up a tide
Using a pole would get you going
Whilst legging with your feet, instead of rowing

The coming of light makes you smile with glee
Like you've never seen it, like you're about to be free
You get down from your back and onto your feet
You wipe your head covered with sweat from the heat
The boat comes out from the tunnel, you step on the land
Then you walk on your feet and feel with your hands.

Rowan Arthur (10)
Durham Road Junior School, Newport

A Magician

A magician lives in a mysterious cellar
Casting evil spells and potions
Wears a metallic purple cloak
Waves a pointed glow in the dark wand
Reads his ancient spell book
Makes monsters to rule the world
Uses glasses to read out of his dark book
His companion is a big black rat
A magician lives in a mysterious cellar.

Fern Gallagher (9)
Durham Road Junior School, Newport

A Magician

A magician lives in an old spooky cellar,
Casting all kinds of different spells,
Wears a red and purple sparkling cloak and hat
Waves a large glittering wand
Reads a miniature black spell book
Makes red, blue and all different colour potions
Uses frogs' legs and snails for brewing his stew
His companion is an evil black cat
A magician lives in an old spooky cellar.

Sam Orphan (9)
Durham Road Junior School, Newport

A Magician

A magician lives in a cold dark cellar
Casting twinkling spells
Wears a glittering spotted hat
Waves a shimmering yellow wand
Reads old dusty books with spells
Makes horrible frogs' leg soup
Uses potions to help him cast his spells
His companion is an old black bat with pointed wings
A magician lives in a cold dark cellar.

Rowan Howard (9)
Durham Road Junior School, Newport

Warriors Of The Cauldron

We are the mighty soldiers of the cauldron
Called back from the grave to make war
We cannot see our families and friends
We cannot turn away from battle
We cannot speak and call out
We are the unwilling warriors who rise from the dead.

Khelsea Jones (9)
Durham Road Junior School, Newport

Snow

A white blanket of ice cream,
Like lumps of candyfloss,
Gleaming icicles,
Sparkling, shimmering
Glittering layers of cotton wool
Footprints in the snow
Like a blue topaz gem
Shining faces with red noses like Rudolph.

Shannen Arnold (10)
Durham Road Junior School, Newport

The Shark Haiku

Teeth like sharp daggers,
Blood-soaked and entrancing eyes
Silent and deadly.

Craig Norvill (11)
Durham Road Junior School, Newport

The Monster

I was going up to bed,
I was feeling scared,
I think I saw a shadow,
I think I saw a head.

I screamed and I screeched,
My mummy came and said,
'There's nothing to be scared of,
There's nothing in your bed.'

But still I felt quite nervous,
But still I wasn't sure,
That a monster was beneath my bed,
Hiding on the floor.

Isabelle Lysaght (9)
Elm Tree House School, Cardiff

My Cats

My cats' names were Suzy and Moses
They were husband and wife
They had a set of kittens
And they were really nice!

The kittens were so pretty
And they were playful too
Black, brown and tabby
I love you!

We found a home for each of them
Loving, warm and kind
I felt so sad to say goodbye
Because they had been mine

Now I don't want any kittens
And Moses left as well
And Suzy seems to come and go
But why I cannot tell

The cat box is now empty
My heart is empty too
I wish I had a kitten
Just like I used to do!

Gabriella Howell (9)
Elm Tree House School, Cardiff

Bugs

I once met an entomologist
I went to his house for tea
There were glass cases of bugs on the walls
Live beetles and flies in balls
Running around with glee
The gnat, the grasshopper, the flea,
One escaped from its box
Crawled inside my socks
I found it in school the next day
And I saw it run away.

Jessica Hodgson (11)
Elm Tree House School, Cardiff

Dragon Death

A knight in shining armour,
Had a sword that shone like gold,
Although it was ancient, it glistened like new,
It had been used by few, but slain so many dragons,
Red, blue, purple, green,
Big, small, fat and lean,
Some were scaly, some were not,
But not one escaped his wrath, no matter what.

Until one day he met his match,
A dragon with an emerald patch,
The knight raised his shield and sword,
The dragon's first flames did nothing at all,
His biggest flame yet lit up the black sky,
Then his wings flapped as he started to fly,
The brave knight stood there looking dumb
And was charred like a hot dog in a bun!

He lifted himself up despite his burns
And continued to fight for all he was worth,
His shield continued to fend off the flames,
But the dragon's attack was not giving way,
The knight's sword flew through the air like a dart
And sat there protruding from the dragon's evil heart,
After that great beast was killed, all others did learn,
'Every dragon's head in the world is what this knight yearns.'

Alexander Harries (11)
Elm Tree House School, Cardiff

The Dragon Of The West

This dragon has glistening, sapphire eyes
With shining, rough blue scales
That splinter the sun
He glides with them majestic wings
That slice the air like a blade through flesh

As the dreaded and mighty dragon of the west
Rampages through Mordor like elephants through a jungle
He kills all in his path and leaves none alive
The land charred and in ruins

The trembling prey of the dragon
Falls limp at the sight of the raging flames, roaring out of
His nose and of his huge, violent talons -
Clawing at this helpless creature of the wild.

The dragon then swoops back down to his lair
Chilly, humid and eerie . . .
With a putrid stench of what could possibly be his dinner!

The evening creeps up into the cave like a robber
Sneaks into a house
The luminous eyes of the dragon light up the gloomy
Cave; lidless and ever-watching

Take heed of my words - don't become foe of
The dragon or who knows in what dire way
He will slaughter you?

Linnéa Freear (10)
Elm Tree House School, Cardiff

The Flying Notes Of My Guitar

A few years ago I played my guitar,
The flying notes travelled afar.
I followed them to my heart's desire,
Until they disappeared in a blaze of fire.

Then I knew the song off by heart,
I heard it so many times.
I didn't know how to start,
Then I learnt a new tune -

The tune was called 'The Blue Moon'.

Now I'm famous for the flying notes of my guitar,
The flying notes that travel afar.
For everyone follows them to their heart's desire,
Until they disappear in a blaze of fire.

Yasmin Wright (9)
Elm Tree House School, Cardiff

My Clothes Have Gone

I'm trying to find my best clothes
But they're not there
Maybe I can wear my shawl
Oh that's not good
But maybe I could wear
My coat with a shiny hood
Oh there's my black shirt
But it's got an orange stain
I'm never going to lose my clothes again
And then I hear some footsteps
My mum is opening the door
'Oh dear, dear little girl
Is this what you're looking for?'

Alysha Leach-Nnadi (8)
Elm Tree House School, Cardiff

Lily

My dog Lily
She is really quite silly,
If you turn your back - it's no good,
She'll greedily snatch your favourite food.

My dog Lily
Is really very silly,
She chases birds into the sea,
Because she fancies them for her tea.

My dog Lily
Is really, really silly,
She licks and she growls,
She has a cheeky little grin
And you know her bite would really sting.

My dog Lily,
She might be silly,
But I love her all the same!

Isabella MacGregor (9)
Elm Tree House School, Cardiff

My Sister

I have a little sister
She's pretty and she's five
I take special care of her
And play with her all the time

And she is really funny
And very, very loving
She is sweet and she's kind
She makes the weather sunny.

Hazen Noell (9)
Elm Tree House School, Cardiff

Fire Bell

Our fire bell does not work
So we tried to have it fixed
But now it goes off every day
So we're sick of it!

We turned our fire bell off one day
Which was a big mistake
For a fire started in the kitchen
When Mummy tried to bake!

The fire flames leapt joyfully
Around the walls and roof
And tried to burn the building down
Now was the moment of truth!

The fire engines turned up at last
To dampen out the flames
Lucky no one was hurt thank goodness
But who was to blame?

So now our fire bell's fixed again
And we are safe and sound
But never tamper with your bell
Or you'll burn your buildings down.

Emily Howell (10)
Elm Tree House School, Cardiff

Peter Rabbit

I love my Peter Rabbit
I've had him since I was born
He sleeps inside a blanket
That's very worn and torn

Peter Rabbit he's the best
Even though he wears a dress
He sleeps in my bed and makes me feel calm
I have sweet dreams when he's lying in my arms.

Sophie Kosinski (10)
Elm Tree House School, Cardiff

Bubblegum

Why is it that bubblegum
Is so tasty?
Is so chewy
Fantastically ooey and gooey?
Smooth like rubber
Pink like a rose -
Stretches so far
Right out to your nose!

Why is it that bubblegum
Wraps around your
Teeth and tongue?
Smells delicious
Such fun to taste
I love blowing bubbles
Sticking it under chairs
Is such a waste!
Bubblegum is so good
I would never forget
About it even if I could!

Robi Fulgoni (9)
Elm Tree House School, Cardiff

Pebbles

You can throw pebbles on the beach
But don't throw mine!
Pebbles you can paint and decorate
But don't throw mine
Mine is special
And you will see
Why he means so much to me
Pebbles is my cat!
No, please don't throw him
How cruel would that be
The RSPCA would soon know about that!

Becky Green (9)
Elm Tree House School, Cardiff

My Mother

You are always there for me, rain, sleet or snow
You tucked me in at night
You taught me how to sew

Whenever I felt poorly you'd stay with me for hours
We'd watch a film together
Called 'Lord Of The Rings, The Two Towers'.

When I came home you'd hug me real tight
I would eat the tea you'd cooked for me
Then my brother and I would fight

I love you Mummy
You are great
Except for when you took my dummy
Why oh why couldn't you wait?

Holly Bickerton (11)
Elm Tree House School, Cardiff

Hippo

A hippo came to tea one day
He came to tea with me
We had a little party
We ate some cake with Smarties

The hippo had good manners
He didn't chew or bite
He ate his food in slow motion
It took him half the night!

And when at last he'd finished
He wiped his mouth and said,
'Thanks, I must get going,
It's time to go to bed!'

Ann-Kathrin Klein (9)
Elm Tree House School, Cardiff

My Family

Now let me see . . .
My dad is a jolly man
He likes his food
My brother is the fighting king
A wiz on the computer
He loves to ride his scooter
My mum is a great cook
Her chocolate cakes are yummy
I love to help her when she bakes
And fill my hungry tummy!
My sister is kind and cool
She keeps an eye on me
She goes to a much bigger school!
This is my lovely family!

Olivia Jarvis (9)
Elm Tree House School, Cardiff

Hallowe'en

Hallowe'en the dead rise,
It is a spooky night,
Step on a crack,
Break your mother's back,
Cross on the stairs and beware!
Break a mirror -
And you're in for a dare!

Witches, skeletons, black cats all around,
Potions brewing, bubbling with sound.

Little children trick or treating,
In the churchyard the ghosts are meeting!

Rose Lubin (10)
Elm Tree House School, Cardiff

My Fish Tank

My fish were called Speedy and Gonzales
They were so fast
They could almost fly
Their tiny blue scales glistened like the blue sky
They were so beautiful and so small
They hardly made a splash at all

They had a castle on the floor
They swim in and out through the grand door
One day my fish looked very ill
I didn't know what to do -
So I flushed them down
The bathroom loo!

Elisabeth Lubin (10)
Elm Tree House School, Cardiff

The Dreams I Have

A dream I had was quite absurd
Funny, weird and mad
I was trapped in a lemon curd
Things went from good to bad

Sometimes I have nightmares
Really scary ones!
One was about a giant bear
Weighing eleven tons

I wonder what gives me these strange dreams
Can it be the cheese?
I think in future for supper
I'll stick to chips and peas!

Caroline Lakin (10)
Elm Tree House School, Cardiff

Fire!

Fire is an angry flame,
Not taking the blame,
Burning anything in its way,
Only water makes it go away.

Colours of yellow, orange and red,
Close your eyes, it's in your head,
It is very hot, it's very wild,
Beware of flames, little child!

Georgina Collins (10)
Elm Tree House School, Cardiff

Footy

Football is my favourite sport,
It is unlike any other sort.
I'd like to play another game,
Even if it is pouring with rain.

When up the field, I dribble the ball,
I concentrate so I don't fall,
A corner is my favourite shot,
When I score, Mum cheers a lot.
Being in goal is a lot of fun,
Because I don't have to run.

Man Utd is my favourite team,
When they score I shout and scream,
Old Trafford is their home ground,
The singing from the fans goes all around,
In a team there are eleven players,
Their formation is in layers.

Harrie Clemens (8)
Hendredenny Park Primary School, Caerphilly

The Ghost Teacher

The school is closed
The sun is down
And every child has gone home without a frown
But there is one person at the school
The lonely teacher
The lonely ghoul
She stands there as clear as glass
Calling out the names of her absent class
She stands alone in the empty room
With no children beside her to her gloom
She tells the empty seats to shut up
While she sips nothing from her white teacup
She walks outside and looks around
Listening to see if she can hear a sound
At the end of school she mutters a word
No one hears, then she picks up her bag
And disappears . . .

Molly Allen (11)
Hendredenny Park Primary School, Caerphilly

Water

When I am happy or see my beautiful daughter,
To remember these things I gaze into water,
The cerulean pools of mystery and love,
Seem like a gift from the heavens above.
I see the lilies and lotuses floating around
And the waterfall making a gushing sound.
Lakes, puddles, oceans, streams,
All look magic when reflecting sunbeams.
They all look beautiful, a delight to admire,
But strong, as it defeats fire.
So next time you're sad, find a lake,
You'll be glad you did, I swear on your sake.

Julia Williams (11)
Hendredenny Park Primary School, Caerphilly

Once Upon A Rhyme

Three little piggies,
Wolf at the door,
He'd had bacon for lunch
And wanted some more.

Three big bears,
Walking in a wood,
Suddenly spotted,
Red Riding Hood.

Along comes Goldilocks,
Hands on her hips,
But here comes the wolf
Licking his lips.

I'd better stop
Before this gets gory,
'Cause after all
It's a fairytale story!

Sam Adamson (10)
Hendredenny Park Primary School, Caerphilly

The Summer Sun

The summer sun
Sits high in the sky
Looking down at me

It warms my face
And colours my skin
So I sit in the shade of a tree

It smiles at the flowers
And I smile too
As I smell the summer breeze

The summer sun
Can mean so much
To all and especially me.

Rhydian Knox (11)
Hendredenny Park Primary School, Caerphilly

Daffodils

All daffodils I see are swaying,
They look like they are playing.

Their petals are always glowing
And they're always flowing.

'Hello,' said a daffodil,
Brightening up his face.

'Oh no,' said another daffodil,
'There's not very much space.'

All the daffodils are very, very weak,
But don't worry, I'll grow some next week.

The next daffodils I planted were very, very strong,
I planted them myself and there's nothing wrong.

Their petals are reflecting off the sun,
All the daffodils your work is done.

Elizabeth New (9)
Hendredenny Park Primary School, Caerphilly

School

Our classroom is very small
In fact the smallest of them all
Loads of girls love to skip
Sometimes we have chicken and chips
At break times everyone plays on the yard
Sometimes our work can be very hard
Loads of boys love football
At assembly everyone goes into the hall
Every week we have singing
On sports day one house ends up winning
Every week we have a spelling test
Everyone tries to do their best.

Charlotte Cavill (10)
Hendredenny Park Primary School, Caerphilly

My Family

My mum is cool
But she doesn't go to school!
She doesn't like slides
Or rides!
She doesn't take sides when me and Katie fight!
I love her and she loves me
That's how it's going to be!

My dad likes rides
And slides!
He is nice
And he doesn't like mice!
I love him, he loves me
That's how it's going to be!

My sister is nice
And she likes mice!
We mostly fight
But we don't fight in the night!
She is cool
And she does go to school!
I love her, she loves me
That's how it's going to be!

Bethan Pugh (10)
Hendredenny Park Primary School, Caerphilly

My Sister

My sister has red hair
Of this you must beware
You will need to take care
If you see her anywhere

My sister is a pest
Although I think she's the best
She nags all day and then all night
But I like it best when she hugs me tight.

Saffron Lloyd (8)
Hendredenny Park Primary School, Caerphilly

Sun

The sun is . . .
a golden candlestick,
burning brightly.

A curved banana,
peeling to give us light.

A bright bulb,
lighting the world.

A beautiful buttercup,
giving pollen to the bees.

A circle of cheese,
resting on a light blue plate.

A warm blanket,
lying over me.

Tirion Stevens (8)
Hendredenny Park Primary School, Caerphilly

Summertime

Summertime fun time
Long days in the sunshine
Playing on the beach
Blue clouds out of reach

Summertime fun time
All day long having a great time
Eating ice cream in the park
Going to bed before it gets dark

Summertime fun time
My very favourite best time
Too soon it comes to an end
Back to school and all my friends.

Alys Lloyd (10)
Hendredenny Park Primary School, Caerphilly

The View

From my little hut I can see the sandy shore with rock pools and shells
And the waves tumbling over the soft wet sand.

From my little hut I can see the clear blue sea frothing and
foaming as the boats go by
And bottlenose dolphins soaring in the sunset.

From my little hut I can see people on surfboards surfing the waves
While children lick ice creams and build sandcastles.

From my flat window I can see tall buildings towering over us,
Casting the city in shadow,
Windows glistening like mirrors in the sun.

From my flat window I can see the streets busy with traffic and
the shop queues as long as a mile.
Pavements packed with tourists and people eating chips on benches.

From my barge window I can see the canal, long and smooth
as if you could walk on it
And the water murky and brown.

From my barge window I can see the grassy banks
With daisies poking through.

From my barge window I can see the great stone bridge
arching over the canal
And the 'Royal Oak' with merry people drinking ale.

Laura Bonar (10)
Hendredenny Park Primary School, Caerphilly

The Ballet Dancer

She leaps in the air
With her hair so fair

She flies up high
Reaching for the sky

She lands gently on the ground
Without a sound

Twisting and turning
With her skirt twirling

She dances like a gentle swan
Gliding through the water
She points her toes
And lifts her arms
And curtsies when it's over.

Rhian Knox (8)
Hendredenny Park Primary School, Caerphilly

The Beach

The sun shone brightly
Glistening through the palm leaves
The clear blue sea sparkled
As it gently broke rolling waves
Onto the golden sand
The breeze was gentle and fresh
Above my head I heard seagulls squawking
As they circled around in the sky
As I walked across the sandy beach
I smelt the luscious smell of candyfloss
The seashells and gritty sand under my feet
Made me walk quicker.

Melissa Palmer (9)
Pantysgallog Primary School, Dowlais

A Day At The Beach

I'm dazzled by the sparkle of the sun
Tiny silvery fish darting in the rock pools

I can smell the sizzling sausages from a beach barbeque
A strong smell of salt from the sea

I can feel the silky soft sand under my bare feet
Icy cold water as it splashed against my feet

I can hear pebbles crunching beneath my feet as I walked
Waves lapping against the sides of the boats.

Robyn Smith (9)
Pantysgallog Primary School, Dowlais

The Beach

I can feel silky soft sand under my feet
And the hot sun blazing down on me

I can see surfers riding the waves
And waves rolling gently to shore

I smell the strong salt sea
The strong powerful smell of seaweed

I can hear children laughing
And pebbles crunching under my feet.

Courtney Barrett (10)
Pantysgallog Primary School, Dowlais

What Am I?

I have no legs
Orange and gold am I
Slow I move
A bowl I live in
I swim all day and night
What am I?

Lucy Evans (10)
Pantysgallog Primary School, Dowlais

What Am I?

Orange, black and white I am
Slowly and swiftly through the long grass
I kill gazelles and kill deer all through the day
Roar, roar, roar I say
What am I?

Jonathan Powell (10)
Pantysgallog Primary School, Dowlais

Cheeky Monkey Haiku

The cheeky monkey
Swinging in the hot jungle
Having lots of fun!

Rebecca Kinsey (9)
Pantysgallog Primary School, Dowlais

The Lazy Puppy Haiku

The lazy puppy,
Lazing in the afternoon,
Out in the backyard.

Abby Evans (9)
Pantysgallog Primary School, Dowlais

Panda Haiku

In China valley
Giant panda chews bamboo
All day, every day!

Julia Astley (10)
Pantysgallog Primary School, Dowlais

The Cheeky Monkey Haiku

The cheeky monkeys
Are searching for bananas
Jumping tree to tree.

Stacey Elliott (10)
Pantysgallog Primary School, Dowlais

The Wolf Haiku

In my backyard grounds
A big wolf cries in anger
Each black starry night.

Jordan Cleaver (10)
Pantysgallog Primary School, Dowlais

My Dumb Cat Haiku

My stupid dumb cat
Sleeps all day and all night long
Dreaming of dinner.

Kyron Sinnett (10)
Pantysgallog Primary School, Dowlais

Chatterbox Haiku

This is a parrot
It is a loud chatterbox
It is just like me.

Lauren Osborne (10)
Pantysgallog Primary School, Dowlais

I Am A . . .

My body is covered in priceless scales,
My skin is a rich eerie green
I swim gently across the still water
I stomp across the dry land
I close my jaws which go *snap*
I live in water and on land
I am the most populous in Australia
I hunt my prey and have them for dinner
I am a pretty reptile
And very sly
What am I?

Tyrion Jones (10)
Pantysgallog Primary School, Dowlais

The King Of Cars

King of the beasts
As fast as lightning am I
Engine roaring like a tiger
Body as red as blood
Wheels as shiny as gold
As swift as a cheetah
Created under Italy's blue skies
I'm a rich man's desire
What am I?

Daniel Lewis (10)
Pantysgallog Primary School, Dowlais

The Rabbit Haiku

In the dark evening,
A rabbit silky stone-grey,
Nibbles a carrot!

Charlotte Johnson (9)
Pantysgallog Primary School, Dowlais

Furry Fluff Ball

I'm furry and cuddly
I can be all different colours
I scurry and whistle
I squeak and chirrup
I live in a cage
Or I live in a hutch
And I nibble and fuss
What am I?

Kirsty Jones (10)
Pantysgallog Primary School, Dowlais

British Icon

I am green as grass
My speed is as fast as light
My expanse is awesome
I growl like a jaguar
My acceleration is blinding
I am a British icon
What am I?

Gavin Llewellyn (10)
Pantysgallog Primary School, Dowlais

What Am I?

I pounce, I leap on velvety paws,
I live in houses or alleys,
My purr sounds like an elderly man snoring,
I am small, fluffy, irresistibly cute,
My little wet nose helps me sniff out my food
And I like to chase butterflies,
What am I?

Catrin Owen (10)
Pantysgallog Primary School, Dowlais

There Was A Young Girl Called Jess!

There was a young girl called Jess
Who had a pretty new dress
She wore it one day
To go out to play
And now it's a terrible mess!

Jessica Jones (10)
Pantysgallog Primary School, Dowlais

The Gypsy Girl

She's always a scruff
And always in a huff
Misty Gyp thinks she's the best
Than all the animals and the rest
She hates the crows
Always last in the row
Always begs for money
All she eats is honey
She always sits at home
All on her own
She never bothers to change
Always in a rage
She's scary
But hairy
Misty Gyp always lies
She never has pies
She always tells the future
She doesn't need a tutor.

Alice Cooksey (9)
Pembroke Primary School, Bulwark

Annastasia Spring

Her face is like a frying pan,
With ears with a suntan,
Her hair is so fair,
She has a wicked smile and a glare.

Here she comes looking very posh,
But look at her ears, she doesn't wash,
'Howdy,' she says, 'Annastasia Spring,'
She thinks she's the king

Annastasia Spring thinks she's the boss,
Why she thinks this, we're at a loss,
So cool, so rich,
But she can't sew a stitch.

She's as bright as a button,
But as tough as a mutton,
She's as strong as an ox,
But as sly as a fox.

She has money to spend,
Though she can't buy a friend,
She looks innocent in the face,
Though really she's a big disgrace.

Megan Kelly (8)
Pembroke Primary School, Bulwark

Elisibeth Lair

The prettiest girl in school is Elisibeth Lair
With her long glowing golden hair
Her smooth perfect skin
Is the hazel colour of gin
Her crisp white clothes
Match her carefully painted toes
Her stockings are white
Like a half-made kite
Her fresh teeth are dentist clean
Making her smile, shimmer and glean
Her mirror-shiny shoes squeak on the floor
While she walks up to the classroom door
Everyone stares at her like they are sleeping
While Timmothy Edwards is busy daydreaming
She is just about mysterious as the sea
But surprisingly she is weirder than me
She knows how to bribe the teacher
That's why she gets a chance to trip up the cleaner
She can hang to a pole like a bat
She is as clever as a cat
Her head is like a half-blown-up balloon
Her lips are as shiny as a new-made spoon
Her pencil case is blue and white
Her dinner money shines like a light
She is a maniac on a computer
So that's why she needs a tutor
So that's Elisibeth Lair with flowing hair.

Sian Cresswell (9)
Pembroke Primary School, Bulwark

Jim, The Bully

There is a nasty bully called Jim
And he'll make your life rather dim
He'll pull your hair
But he doesn't care
And he'll punch you in
And kick your shin
He is quite big
He wears a wig
His hair is quite brown
He will make you frown
He is quite plump
And he's a big grump
His totally huge lips
Look like big red chips
He is not fair
He doesn't share
He will lie
And make you cry
He has very weird eyes
Like very big flies
He will rant and rave
And you'll be his slave
He has large ears
Like cans of beers
When you write
He'll start a fight
He's a fighting machine
And he's really mean
He's 9 years old,
He's rather bold.

Keiran Jones (9)
Pembroke Primary School, Bulwark

All About Naughty Ned And Silly Sam

Naughty Ned thinks he's cool,
His frightful behaviour's dreadful in school,
Naughty Ned has hair gel at the front,
He always makes an enormous grunt,
Naughty Ned isn't pretty at all,
He always ends up looking like a fool,
Naughty Ned lives at Dragon Drive,
Naughty Ned is only five.

There is also a girl called Silly Sam,
She doesn't even weigh a gram,
Silly Sam wears a golden dress,
But she always makes a lot of mess,
Silly Sam has golden shoes,
They look like big horse's hooves,
She also puts a smile on your face,
It is never a big disgrace,
Silly Sam's hair is shiny, brown and curly,
But she wishes her hair was nice, blonde and swirly.

Cody Frowen (9)
Pembroke Primary School, Bulwark

Sam Johns

Sam Johns likes to eat beef,
Using his chipped and grimy teeth,
He is very, very poor,
He can't even afford a door,
Sam John's teacher is a ghoul,
He scared his class away, what a fool,
Sam Johns walks to school,
To find his headmaster's a mule,
Sam Johns has a big nose,
He smells from head to toes,
Sam Johns likes to play cricket,
Although he's used as the wicket,
Sam Johns' friend is called Mike,
Mike really likes to ride his bike,
His hair is very curly,
He thinks it's pretty girly,
Sam Johns is as thin as a rake,
Funny that because he eats lots of cake,
Sam Johns likes watching Scooby Doo
Winnie the Pooh, Mr Magoo and Doctor Who.

William Thomas (9)
Pembroke Primary School, Bulwark

Jane The Pain

My friend Jane is extremely tall
Her head is as big as a giraffe's zoo stall
She goes in a shop on a wedding day
And she didn't come out until May
When she came out, she was in pain
Because she got hit by a big yellow crane
She went to the hospital to see what was the matter
And then they said that her finger was made out of batter
Jane went to school on Sunday
And realised it was school on Monday
My mate Jane was so sad
So I bought her, her favourite yellow pad
My mate Jane was late for school
All because of a game of pool
Jane was a worker at a shop
She chewed some bubblegum and it went pop
Jane bought some shiny shoes
Went to the pub for some booze
Jane is very stupid, she can't even find a shop
She won't stop laughing and then she went pop.

Emma Skidmore (9)
Pembroke Primary School, Bulwark

My Bigger Bully

Her face is like a big white bowl
And her stomach is a big black hole
She always thinks she's tough
But never bad or terribly rough
Everyone says she's fat and tall
But she's really thin and small
Her arms are like two fat snakes
Her legs are like thin brown rakes
Her hair is like 100 wires
Sticking out of two big tyres
Her ears are like two big tools
Her eyes are like two round shaped pools
She may be scary and sad
But that's no reason to be bad
Her heart is as cold as snow
She's frightening and scary and her big eyes glow
Everyone thinks she's big and strong
But really she is small and long
She's always being bad
But is really lonely and sad.

Kayla Viljoen (9)
Pembroke Primary School, Bulwark

Marigold

She has ears like seashells
She rings her little bells
She has eyes like pools
And her hair is cool
She gets bullied by Barry
She doesn't like Larry
She has hair like a loo brush
She has things that are lush
She has a mouth like a head
She knows people who are dead
Her belly is thin
She puts everything in the bin
Her classroom is like a cube
She has a friend, Rube
Her glasses are like bottle tops
She likes to watch Top Of The Pops
She never speaks
She always peeks.

Hannah Polhill (9)
Pembroke Primary School, Bulwark

Patrick Star

Patrick Star walks to school
His head as big as a swimming pool
Ears as round as circle rings
Teeth rust like worn out bins
His shoes have holes where his toes poke through
His nose is cold and often blue
He wears a rustic hat
And he smells like an old tomcat
He's got a sister called Sally
Who lives in Rhonda Valley
He tells everybody he flew to the moon
But we know he didn't, he was back too soon
They say he lived in a castle fit for a king
He owned a lot of gold and a big diamond ring
They say he was married to a beautiful wife
She went away and left him and ruined his life
He searches the streets every day
He can't find her, she went away.

Robbie Fisher (9)
Pembroke Primary School, Bulwark

Carly Louise

Carly Louise is my best friend
Our friendship never ends
Carly had lots of fun
After she had an iced bun
She has lovely light brown hair
And she's got a little teddy bear
Carly is mad
It's not often you see her sad
Carly would like a poodle
But will settle for a pot noodle
Carly uses a mop and broom
To tidy up her bedroom
Carly loves ice cream
When it's cold she might scream
When it was time for bed
Carly bumped her head
Carly once climbed a tree
But fell out when she was stung by a bee
Carly was using a printer
And somehow she managed to get a splinter.

Gemma Hall (9)
Pembroke Primary School, Bulwark

Tommy Tiddles

Tommy Tiddles likes his school
But he also wished he had a pool

Tommy Tiddles likes his beef
If he doesn't get any, he'll break your teeth

Tommy Tiddles has grimy teeth
And is a very charming thief

Tommy Tiddles can't take a joke
And only talks to his family folk

Tommy Tiddles is very skinny
Just like his sister little Ginny

Tommy Tiddles is poor and smelly
And has no food in his belly

Tommy Tiddles thinks he's the best
But he always stands out to the rest

Tommy Tiddles loves the summer
And his dad is a very good drummer

Tommy Tiddles throws stones
I hope he doesn't break my bones

Tommy Tiddles always wiggles
He can't help it if he fiddles.

Jack Bevan (9)
Pembroke Primary School, Bulwark

Make Me A . . .

I am only a puddle make me a sea
I am only a seed make me a tree
I am only a child make me a man
I am only paper make me a fan
I am only ink make me a pen
I am only a feather make me a wren
I am only lead make me a pencil
I am only a ruler make me a stencil
I am only a page make me a book
I am only a meal make me a cook
I am only metal make me steel
I am only rubber make me a wheel
I am only wool make me a rug
I am only china make me a jug
I am only a brick make me a house
I am only a sparrow make me a grouse
I am only tar make me a road
I am only small make me a load
I am only an engine make me a car
I am only a boy help me go far.

Freddie Jones (11)
Pendoylan CW Primary School, Cowbridge

A Witch's Spell

Double double, toil and trouble
Eye of newt and mink's tail
Stir it round and add a whale's tail
An eye of pig, a rabbit's head
But make sure it's dead
This is all I need for my spell
And it will make you feel like you're in Hell.

Matthew Popham (11)
Pendoylan CW Primary School, Cowbridge

A Witch's Spell

Fizzle, fizzle, toil and bake,
Let the cauldron burn and shake.
Drop in a dead man's toe,
A slimy snake and some dirty toads.

A fish's eye, a bat's wing,
A lock of hair and a bird that sings.
A drop of magic shall do the trick,
Then get your spoon, give it a mix.

Take a young dragon's scale,
Then pinch a bit of the dangerous gale.
Then mix it till it is thick,
Let it turn green in a tick.

Fizzle, fizzle, toil and bake,
Let the cauldron burn and shake.
This is a spell that shall only be told,
To all the witches within a book they hold.

Megan Phillips (11)
Pendoylan CW Primary School, Cowbridge

A Witch's Spell

Sizzle, fizzle, mix and shake
Slugs and bats can be baked
A big fat boil from a wizard's chin

Sizzle, fizzle, mix and shake
A dead python from the lake
Some cuckoo spit from the tree
No one in this world is ever free from me.

Millicent Jenkins (11)
Pendoylan CW Primary School, Cowbridge

Wales

I'm proud to be Welsh,
I feel like Wales is all mine,
That always sends shivers down my spine,
We have so many stories and tales,
The Welsh play rugby and never fail,
That makes me proud to be Welsh.

Farmers keep cattle and sheep,
I could listen to the chorus till I sleep,
Our emblem is the leek and daffodils,
People come to see mountain and hills,
There are still some mines that people see,
There is beautiful countryside with very old trees.

This is the place people should be and see,
Wales is the place not to be missed,
There's always something good on Wales' list.

Paisley Orchard-Brown (10)
Pendoylan CW Primary School, Cowbridge

A Witch's Spell

Sizzle gizzle, stir and bake,
Put it in the cauldron and give it a shake.

Put in some rat's blood and its bones,
Mix that together with some stones.

An eye of a snake and a crocodile's tail,
Mix that together then add a snail.

Take all the organs out of a frog,
Mix that together with an eyeball from a dog.

Sizzle gizzle, stir and bake,
This is the best spell I can make.

Ella Sylvester (10)
Pendoylan CW Primary School, Cowbridge

War/Peace

War!
Why does war start?
Why does war break hearts?
Why does war create strife?
Why does a bullet take away a life?
Why do corpses fill the fields
With poppy-covered guns and shields?

Peace
Peace is like an angel
Floating high above,
Dodging all the bad things
But searching for love.
Peace is like a dove
Without a single sin,
Stretching out its feathers
And blessing every kin.

Hannah Ballinger (11)
Pendoylan CW Primary School, Cowbridge

Peace Poem

Peace is an angel
Bring love and trust
Peace is an angel
Bring love and kindness
Peace is an angel
Bring silence and joy
Peace is an angel
Bring respect and forgiveness.

Ryan Hawkins (11)
Pendoylan CW Primary School, Cowbridge

The Cave

A cave is nestled in the mountain tops,
Out comes a roar that never stops.

In the hole he lies there,
Spreading illness and fear.

A brave knight rides up the hill,
Ready to attack, ready to kill.

He reaches and grabs the sword,
If he kills the dragon he becomes lord.

In he goes, wary and scared,
He knows if he gets it wrong, he is dead.

The dragon pounces onto him,
They made a very awful din.

In the end only one can win,
The one who ended all the din.

The one with eyes that shone like red-hot fires,
The one whose roar never tires.

Patrick O'Brien (10)
Pendoylan CW Primary School, Cowbridge

The Witch

The witch was flying high in the midnight sky,
She wears a black cloak and she is very, very sly.
Her eyes are green and red bloodshot,
Her teeth so black can easily rot,
She has a pet cat for her slave,
She lives in a dark old hole of a cave,
She can make potions like never before,
She has to do it, it's the witch's law.

Jordan Guard (10)
Pendoylan CW Primary School, Cowbridge

Dream Worlds

I close my eyes and then I see
A snow-white unicorn in front of me

Suddenly I lift up towards the sky
I land on the unicorn and it starts to fly

We fly so high up into the light
Of the fantastic stars that shine so bright

I look below and suddenly
A different world in front of me

The colours we get close to, down we go
They go so neatly like a river's flow

A different world in front of me
The mountains so high, grey and rocky

The sheep on the hills with their little white tails
The unicorn swoops and then it fails

I fall and feel I'm going to die
But before I hit the ground, I open one eye.

Lowri Davies (10)
Pendoylan CW Primary School, Cowbridge

What Is War?

What is war? Is it something that kills
Or is it something that gives you thrills?

What is war? Does it make you terrified
Or does it make you full of pride?

What is war? Is it awful
Or is it pretty and delightful?

What is war? Does it make you as cold as ice
Or does it make you warm and nice?

Clementine Haines (11)
Pendoylan CW Primary School, Cowbridge

War

Men whose faces are twisted by hate
All know their destined fate

Many families have suffered pain
From the beginning of wars to Saddam Hussein

Poppies stand in fields
But families' hearts can never be healed

Soldiers who are so brave
For victory so many of them crave

In the street people go by
Some of them even cry

Then in a rainbow comes peace
But families have been hurt never the least.

Caitlin Sturgess-Webb (10)
Pendoylan CW Primary School, Cowbridge

War

Why does war cause so much pain?
People start wars like Saddam Hussein

Soldiers are so mean
Iraqis are killed at sixteen

People die in the big bad war
They crawl in the bloody gore!

Dropping bombs and huge missiles
You can even look in the military files

Shells are flying over our heads
People are lying in their deathbeds

The war is over there's been no fun
Please don't start another one.

Kentaro Abe-Donovan (10)
Pendoylan CW Primary School, Cowbridge

Pirates

Watch out because here they come,
Pirates screaming even if they're dumb.

With their swords in one hand and nothing in the other,
Their teeth are black, they have wild looks, they're mad.

A parrot on one shoulder and too much gold,
Sometimes they're hairy and sometimes they're bald.

They wear lots of jewellery and lots of velvet.

They steal medallions and valuable stuff,
Now don't be fooled, they are a bit tough

Now this is the time they are off to their homes,
Now they go and cut throats, while they sail on their boats.

Louisa Bryant (10)
Pendoylan CW Primary School, Cowbridge

Mary Tudor - Heartbroken

I write my diary all day,
Not thinking of my father far away,
With his new wife Anne Boleyn,
Beautiful, but full of sin.

I do want my mother back here on Earth,
So she could comfort me, like when she gave me birth.
But now she's gone, my heart's full of pain,
Knowing I won't see her again.

Now my heart is hollow,
Brain confused, not knowing which path to follow,
I sit in this castle alone,
Wishing and wanting to go back home.

Hasminder Aulakh (9)
Pendoylan CW Primary School, Cowbridge

A Day On The Farm

A day on the farm is all we need,
Uncle John's started planting hay seed,
Come on, get out of bed,
Come on, hurry up you sleepyhead.

Aunt Jo's just got out of bed,
She's planning to make a loaf of bread,
Come on, get out of bed,
Come on, hurry up you sleepyhead.

The tractor's stored in the barn
And cousin Ruth is spinning some yarn,
Come on, get out of bed,
Come on, hurry up you sleepyhead.

Mum and Dad have just left Spain,
Cousin Dan's broken her arm again,
Come on get out of bed,
Come on, hurry up you sleepyhead.

Cousin Kate is down in the lane,
Grooming her little pony's mane,
Come on get out of bed,
Come on, hurry up you sleepyhead.

Mollie Sturgess-Webb (10)
Pendoylan CW Primary School, Cowbridge

Dragon

This creature is the biggest of them all,
He lives in a cave which is so tall,
Knights try to kill it with their swords,
This creature blows fire which is tremendous
And he kills them all,
This creature is a legend no one knows why,
People just think it's all a lie,
The dragon is the best of them all,
Because he is so fearsome and so tall.

Michael Bryant (10)
Pendoylan CW Primary School, Cowbridge

Bad Spell

A frog's leg will do
A bit of rabbit for the stew

Round and round
The cauldron I go

A fish's head
A snake that is dead

Round and round
The cauldron I go

A bit of poison
Will do just fine

Round and round
The cauldron I go.

Ben Borbas (10)
Pendoylan CW Primary School, Cowbridge

The Magic Box

(Based on 'Magic Box' by Kit Wright)

I will put in the box . . .
A nice fluffy teddy
With a nice fur coat

I will put in the box . . .
A sparkling star
And a chick hatching out of an egg

I will put in the box . . .
A shiny fireman
And my bible story book.

Callum O'Brien (7)
Pendoylan CW Primary School, Cowbridge

War

Why war?
Disaster in store!

A single knife
Can take a life!

People conquering land
I think it should be banned!

Why do hearts break?
When bloody corpses lie in the lake!

Guns and shields
Lie in the battlefields!

Battlefield covered with blood
Dying people in the mud!

All war causes is pain and devastation,
Through the whole wide world in every single nation!

Fear and glory in the air
I wish peace would come and make it fair!

People lie in their beds waiting to die,
As armies march into their homes, they just happen to cry!

Rhiannan Falshaw-Skelly (10)
Pendoylan CW Primary School, Cowbridge

Good Spell

Magic beams of light
What a very good sight
Love from a bow
Same colours from a rainbow
And a sprinkle of snow
Maybe a heart or even two
Add unicorns and a beautiful sunrise so rare
Magic beams of light
And now my spell is full of delight.

Amanda Mohabir (10)
Pendoylan CW Primary School, Cowbridge

When I Was . . .

When I was one
I had only begun.
When I was two
I felt quite new.
When I was three
I hurt my knee.
When I was four
I could open the door.
When I was five
I felt so alive.
When I was six
I liked playing with sticks.
When I was seven
I thought I was in Heaven.
When I was eight
I swung on the gate.
When I was nine
I felt quite fine.

Angharad Jane Roberts Wall (9)
Pendoylan CW Primary School, Cowbridge

Dracula's Castle

It's standing there in the dark,
A streak of lightning, a werewolf's bark.
No one knows what lurks inside,
Dr Jekyll or Mr Hyde?
There's shrieks of pain like someone's killing,
Evil vampires finding it thrilling,
But somewhere in there lurking around,
Dracula's in there fighting for ground.
I know the truth, I know it well,
One day Dracula, you're going to Hell.

Charlie Morgan-Ivey (10)
Pendoylan CW Primary School, Cowbridge

My Nightmare

One night in my bed,
Some scary things entered my head.

For one minute there was nothing,
Then suddenly came the scare like a sudden ting.

There were zombies, mummies and ghouls,
Throwing me into this place, *scare school*.

All of the creepy scares, scare me in my head,
I try to say it's not true but I feel I'm about to be dead.

The horrible creatures that I most hate,
They always come to me when the hour is late.

Now it's an early time,
For the rest of the day, I'll be fine.

Joel Gehler (9)
Pendoylan CW Primary School, Cowbridge

Horses

Horses are usually quite tame,
As they gallop around they know they reign,
They move down fields knowing they won't yield,
So they end up with fame.
Horses are also quite greedy,
Snatching for more, neighing feed me.
They wrestle off packets making such a racket
And they get a big telling off!
Horses' tails and manes are so long,
They could nearly touch a plane,
With a flick of a tail, the pain couldn't fail
And the nastiest are the males.

Katherine Gray (10)
Pendoylan CW Primary School, Cowbridge

The Supply Teacher

Our teacher has a sore throat,
She went on a sailor's boat.
And swallowed too much salt water.
Now we have a supply teacher,
Her old job was a preacher,
Her English lessons are a bore,
As for her maths lessons, they're a chore.
We have to be absolutely *silent!*
She has a pointer like a trident.
If you just ask for a rubber,
She'll shout so loud, she'll make you blubber.
I guess she can't be all that bad,
No, what am I saying? She's totally mad!

Helen Needs (9)
Pendoylan CW Primary School, Cowbridge

New Kid In School

A new kid in school, what, no way!
On our waiting list she'll have to stay.
But here she is as true as can be!
My friends were not joking, now I can see.
She comes, what? A Dracula school bag!
I can't quite see her name tag.
I'll go over and ask what it is,
I found out her name, it is Liz.
She's going to be here for a while,
She seems to look at me and break a smile.
She is quite cool, yeah she is,
She is now my best friend, Liz.

Martha Reed (9)
Pendoylan CW Primary School, Cowbridge

Animal Poem

Big wings beating,
Golden feathers shining,
Searching for food,
Claw-shaped beak,
Strong ripping talons,
Sleek movements through the air,
Little head, big body,
Sharp eyesight, great for spotting prey,
What am I?

Macsen McCarthy (9)
Pendoylan CW Primary School, Cowbridge

Animal Poem

Black and orange stripes
Enemy of the lion
Very fierce
Loud, big roar
Big mouth, giant jaw
Hunting for food
Living in the jungle
Roar!

Tomos Kamal (9)
Pendoylan CW Primary School, Cowbridge

Rusty

My friend is Rusty
I love my friendly pony
We gallop through the fierce wind
We jump over the hungry hedges
I love my pony.

Cerys Davis-Greene (9)
Pendoylan CW Primary School, Cowbridge

Who Am I?

I have four paws,
Jaws and claws.
I'm black and white,
I never bite.
I beg and lick,
I feel sorry for humans, when they're sick.
I chew on bones,
I like to play with stones,
Who am I?

Sophie Vellam (9)
Pendoylan CW Primary School, Cowbridge

Animal Poem

Rough tongue lapping
Sharp green eyes blinking
Out all night
Little paws padding
Small ears pricked
Sleek golden fur
Long tail swaying
Who am I?

Emily Groves (8)
Pendoylan CW Primary School, Cowbridge

Who Am I?

White teeth gleaming in the sun
Crouching down, getting ready to pounce
Glossy mane shaking as it tears apart its prey
Heart pounding as it rests
Claws out, ready to do it again
Who am I?

Eliza Hogg (9)
Pendoylan CW Primary School, Cowbridge

Animal Poem

Long tail waving
Sharp teeth shining
Dark stripy skin
Cross voice growling
Black eyes staring
Small orange ears
Four fast legs
Small black nose
Meat-eating animal
Living in India
What am I?

Rachel Harman (9)
Pendoylan CW Primary School, Cowbridge

A Summer Acrostic

S is for the sun that shines bright in the sky
U is for umbrella, that we sit under on the beach
M is for melting, that the sun does to our ice cream
M is for music, that the birds sing
E is for everybody playing outside
R is for roses, growing really tall.

Huw Beynon (9)
Pendoylan CW Primary School, Cowbridge

Poem

P is for poems which can be such fun
O is for originality for poems old and new
E is for excellent poems we read
M is for magic that poems can be.

James Hendy (9)
Pendoylan CW Primary School, Cowbridge

I Love My Dog

I have a dog
Who plays around with a ball and rolls in a bog
A dog which we take for walks and a dog which talks
He fell in a moat and got picked up by a boat
Now he has a chocolate-brown fur coat
My friend is funny and once chased a bunny
He never growls and always fouls
He doesn't bite and likes to chase my kite
I love my dog because he is fun and loves to roll around in the sun.

Elinor Wilby (9)
Pendoylan CW Primary School, Cowbridge

My Best Friend

My best friend is not a person or a hound,
It has four legs that gallop along the ground,
My best friend has a chestnut face with a white stripe going
down the face,
She is very gentle in every way,
My best friend is not a person or a hound,
My best friend is better than I can say!

Jessica Baber (9)
Pendoylan CW Primary School, Cowbridge

Summer

Summer is . . .
Hot, sizzling barbecues
Melting ice cream
Long hot walks
Sweet strawberries
Summer is everything to me.

Martha Bickerton (5)
Pendoylan CW Primary School, Cowbridge

Animal Poem

Shiny grey fur, smooth and short
Pounding along with a long pink tongue
With blazing eyes glaring ahead
A snarl and a pant
A crouch of the head
I jump and I bound
I growl and I howl
And stay by your side
And get a nice bed
I'm a dog of course
With an owner I'm led.

Alana Wilson (9)
Pendoylan CW Primary School, Cowbridge

Sounds

The tiniest sound in the world must be
Ants walking up and down a tree
The spookiest sound in the world must be
A witch singing songs with its cat in a tree
The noisiest sound in the world must be
The waves in the sea crashing over me
The happiest sound in the world must be
The birds singing in a hollow tree.

Rhys Morgan (7)
Pendoylan CW Primary School, Cowbridge

Summer

Summer is . . .
Colourful flowers
Cold, creamy ice cream
Sizzling, sticky sausages
Red, juicy strawberries.

Evan Stafford (6)
Pendoylan CW Primary School, Cowbridge

Big Hairy Monster

My dog is a monster
She eats flies
She has lots of wrinkles
Which don't look nice
She snores in the night
She fights with the light
Oh why is my dog so heavy?
She eats apples
And sucks on oranges
She can't fit through doors
Oh why is my dog so fat?

Gus McPherson (9)
Pendoylan CW Primary School, Cowbridge

Colours
(Based on 'Magic Box' by Kit Wright)

I will put in the box . . .
Blue for the sky,
Yellow for the jelly,
Green for the grass.

I will put in the box . . .
Brown for the mud,
White for a polar bear,
Red for the blood.

Louis Hughes (6)
Pendoylan CW Primary School, Cowbridge

Summer

Summer is
Colourful flowers
Sizzling, sticky sausages
Sticky cool ice cream
Nice hot walks.

Douglas Wilson (6)
Pendoylan CW Primary School, Cowbridge

What's In The Sea?

What's in the sea? What's in the sea?
Six shiny chubby fish looking at me
What's in the sea? What's in the sea?
Three gloomy fish in front of me
What's in the sea? What's in the sea?
Two little dolphins splashing at a palm tree
What's in the sea? What's in the sea?
Mermaids swimming with me.

Annabel Smith (6)
Pendoylan CW Primary School, Cowbridge

Sounds

The tiniest sound in the world must be
My little nice goldfish bubbling in front of me
The spookiest sound in the world must be
The little dog howling by the tree
The noisiest sound in the world must be
The fire alarm, it is really scary
The happiest sound in the world must be
My cat purring gently.

Rachael Hutchings (7)
Pendoylan CW Primary School, Cowbridge

Our Book

The tiniest sound must be
An ant eating its tea.
The spookiest sound must be
The bell ringing in Hell,
The noisiest sound must be
A storm putting hills down on knees
The happiest sound must be
Our baby playing with me!

Peter Bryant (7)
Pendoylan CW Primary School, Cowbridge

Diamonds And Butterflies

I have a blue, red and yellow diamond
Can you see?
A shimmering reflection
Shining at me.

I look up in the sky
What do I see?
A big colourful butterfly
Looking at me.

Olivia Shah (7)
Pendoylan CW Primary School, Cowbridge

Colours

Red is a volcano exploding!
Blue is the waves on the sea.
Green is the grass waving in the wind.
Yellow is the sun in the sky.
Brown is a coconut, I like the juice inside.
Orange is a nice orange for me to eat.
White is my shirt.
Black is a limo
With a very important person inside.

Tomos Rae (7)
Pendoylan CW Primary School, Cowbridge

Sounds

The tiniest sound in the world must be
A bird landing on a tree.
The spookiest sound in the world must be
The boiler cackling like a witch in a tree.
The noisiest sound in the world must be
The waves crashing in the sea.
The happiest sound in the world must be
The birds singing in the breeze.

Natasha Sahonte (7)
Pendoylan CW Primary School, Cowbridge

Colours

Red is a volcano exploding.
Blue is the language book.
Brown is the ruler because it is made of wood.
Grey is a donkey,
Gold is the money in my pocket.
Green is the grass waving in the wind.
Yellow is my word boo.
White is a cup that I drink out of.
Black is the night sky when I fall asleep.
Orange is an orange so sweet.

Alex Guard (7)
Pendoylan CW Primary School, Cowbridge

The Magic Box

(Based on 'Magic Box' by Kit Wright)

I will put in the box . . .
A shiny Game Boy
And shiny shoes
And a special key.

I will put in the box . . .
A frog that will turn into a prince
A magic book of spells
A magic wand
A sparkling light.

Thomas Austin (7)
Pendoylan CW Primary School, Cowbridge

Summer

Summer is . . .
Sizzling barbeques
Melting ice cream
Soaking my sister with water.

Harry Thomas (6)
Pendoylan CW Primary School, Cowbridge

What's In The Sea?

What's in the sea?
What's in the sea?
Green seaweed as green as can be.
What's in the sea?
What's in the sea?
A great big shiny dolphin looking at me.
What's in the sea?
What's in the sea?
The small fish are swimming as far as I can see.
What's in the sea?
What's in the sea?
An orange starfish lying in the weeds.

Hannah Porch (7)
Pendoylan CW Primary School, Cowbridge

Summer Is . . .

Summer is . . .
Lovely colourful flowers
Diving in the sea
Lovely cold ice cream
Red juicy strawberries.

Thomas Orr (6)
Pendoylan CW Primary School, Cowbridge

Summer

Summer is . . .
Silky dresses
Beautiful colourful sunset
Crunchy apples
Sweet grass.

Emma Popham (6)
Pendoylan CW Primary School, Cowbridge

Colours

Blue is the colour in the sea.
Red is my fluffy pillow.
Green is my crunchy apple.
Yellow is my lovely banana.
Brown is my wooden door.
Black is the dark night.
White is the colour of my wall.
Pink is the colour of my shirt.
Orange is the colour of my socks.
Purple is my mum's favourite colour.
Grey is the colour of a rainy day.
Silver is the colour of a diamond.
Gold is the colour of treasure.

Jonathan Mitchell (7)
Pendoylan CW Primary School, Cowbridge

Summer

Summer is . . .
Melting ice cream
Hot barbeques
Cool paddling pool
Long sunny days.

Amelia Sylvester (6)
Pendoylan CW Primary School, Cowbridge

Summer

Summer is . . .
Hot sizzling pies
Cool minty ice cream
Beautiful butterflies
Tall sandcastles.

Alicia Archer (5)
Pendoylan CW Primary School, Cowbridge

War

Adults are screaming, children are crying,
As they can hear the soldiers' guns firing.
Everyone is petrified,
As most of their family has probably died.

There's chaos and hatred in the air,
Why can't we all just be fair?
The soldiers are ducking, always alert,
Their bodies are covered in blood and dirt.

Men are being killed while fighting in the war,
Children are screaming at what they just saw.
War is chaos, war is violent,
When the destroying is done everything is silent.

Jade Riggs (10)
Pendoylan CW Primary School, Cowbridge

Summer

Summer is . . .
Red juicy strawberries
Colourful pretty plants
Cold creamy ice cream
Cold paddling pools.

Louisa Knowles (6)
Pendoylan CW Primary School, Cowbridge

Summer

Summer is . . .
Beautiful colourful flowers
Sticky creamy ice cream
Cool paddling pools
Fresh sweet grass.

Megan Bradwick (5)
Pendoylan CW Primary School, Cowbridge

A Witch's Curse!

Double, double, boil and bubble,
Crush his bones, cause him trouble,
Curse his body, take his soul,
From start to end we'll have our goal!

Double, double, toil and trouble,
Make his bones a pile of rubble,
Take his oranges, one by one,
Cause him pain, make it fun!

Curse him! Curse him, stir his mind,
Take his eyeballs, make him blind,
Curse his soul, curse his sin,
We're finished now, away with him!

Taya Mouncher (11)
Pendoylan CW Primary School, Cowbridge

Summer

Summer is . . .
Mint flavoured ice cream
Different coloured flowers
Picking juicy strawberries
Hot sandy beaches.

Sam Aston (5)
Pendoylan CW Primary School, Cowbridge

Summer

Summer is . . .
Beautiful butterflies
Long green grass
Long sunset
Rolling down hills.

Ffion Smith (6)
Pendoylan CW Primary School, Cowbridge

Wales

Wales, Wales where I want to be,
Sights and scenes you just have to see.
We have our castles and our mines too,
Buildings and countryside, the perfect view.

Welsh sport is on a high,
We score many a goal and many a try.
The national anthem, will show us who we are,
The dragon, the daffodil, the leek and St David's Day takes us far.

Wales is forever true,
The passion is there, in me and you.
The country of Wales will stick in your mind,
It is the best country you will ever find.

James Wakely (11)
Pendoylan CW Primary School, Cowbridge

Summer

Summer is . . .
Cold ice cream
Diving in pools
Hot sandy beaches
Sleeping in the sun.

Alexander Lloyd (6)
Pendoylan CW Primary School, Cowbridge

Summer

Summer is . . .
Lovely long walks
Beautiful colourful flowers
Melting creamy ice cream.

Johanna Little (5)
Pendoylan CW Primary School, Cowbridge

Good Spell

Round and round the cauldron I go
Magic bean and petals slow

Bluebells in fields and doves in trees
Everything lovely I cannot believe

Hair from a king and a ring from a queen
Lovely diamonds that have never been seen

Just a sprinkle of fairy dust
And a heap of trust

Just one more thing, in the cauldron it goes
Just a petal from a very nice rose.

Evie Amos (10)
Pendoylan CW Primary School, Cowbridge

Summer

Summer is . . .
Melting ice cream
Hot burgers
Tasty sweet strawberries
Cold paddling pools.

Harry Horan (5)
Pendoylan CW Primary School, Cowbridge

Summer Haiku

A hot sunny day
Jumping on my trampoline
That's what summer is!

Curtis Browning (6)
Pendoylan CW Primary School, Cowbridge

War

War is a horrible thing,
People are dying for their king.

People are full of fear,
Because war is here.

Guns in hand,
Aeroplanes starting to land.

People are hurt,
Covered in dirt.

People are shouting and screaming,
Eyes are beaming.

Now the war has to die,
There will be no more bullets or smoke in the sky.

Molly Westlake (10)
Pendoylan CW Primary School, Cowbridge

Summer

Summer is hot sizzling sausages on a barbeque
Fresh colourful flowers and grass
Cold melting ice creams
Hot sandy beaches
Cool, warm paddling pools.

Aniella Perrins (6)
Pendoylan CW Primary School, Cowbridge

Summer

Summer is . . .
Hot nice barbeques
Colourful flowers
Building small sandcastles
Red lovely strawberries.

Ellie Davies (5)
Pendoylan CW Primary School, Cowbridge

My Box Of Treasures

(Based on 'Magic Box' by Kit Wright)

I will put in the magical box . . .
A golden diamond ring on my pink finger,
An everlasting skiing holiday in Albach
And a silver Hickstead Derby cup
Shining in my pink hand.

I will put in the magical box . . .
A hard clay pot I made by myself on a boring wet day,
A smell of my favourite foods on my brightly coloured plate
And a tiny black purring kitten.

I will put in the magical box . . .
A song singing about magical colours glowing on a piece of paper,
A glorious football match being won by Wales in the
                                        noisy Millennium Stadium
And a beautiful black horse galloping in a field.

Charlotte Prichard (l8)
Pendoylan CW Primary School, Cowbridge

War

Death creeps over the battlefield,
Your fate is sealed,
Can you see the distraught transfixed stare in the soldiers' eyes?
You are but a child traumatised.
You and others will fight till the cannon of death erupts in your face.
You know you have no chance against the deadly mace.
Your deathbed awaits you.
It will give no warning or alarming sound.
Your deathbed you will find is soft, poppy-covered ground.
Like a quilted cloud.
Goodbye to you who are doomed to die.

Thea Young (11)
Pendoylan CW Primary School, Cowbridge

Funny Poem

(Based on 'Down Behind The Dustbin' by Michael Rosen)

Down behind the dustbin
I met a dog called Sid
He could smell a bone inside
But couldn't lift the lid.

Down behind the dustbin
I met a dog called Ted
Putting on his pyjamas
And going to his bed.

Down behind the dustbin
I met a dog called Jack
He said, 'I'm going to New Zealand
I really have to pack.'

Down behind the dustbin
I met a dog called Bert
He was wearing a hair bobble
And he was putting on a skirt.

Christopher Gray (8)
Pendoylan CW Primary School, Cowbridge

Fireworks

We hear the fireworks in the sky,
We hear them scream and loudly cry,
See their lovely ruby showers,
Watch them spread their sparkling powers,
We taste the burning of their sizzle,
We smell their strong smoky wizzle,
The smell of smoke is in the air,
Fireworks sometimes give a scare,
They spin and twirl
And whizz and whirl!
Watch their beauty as they unfurl!

Imogen Humphreys (11)
Pendoylan CW Primary School, Cowbridge

Wales

Wales has the sparkling sand
Wales has the peaceful shore,
So come down to Wales
And you'll be begging to see some more!

Our scenes and sights are wonderful
And our tales will thrill your mind,
In Wales there's surely nothing
That you cannot find.

Our mountains so tall,
Our valley so deep,
The countryside so spacious
Filled with cattle and sheep.

Listen to us singing,
Come and watch us dance,
Our history and castles
Will put you in a trance.

Even though we have had bad gales
The place to be is surely Wales!
So sing our anthem loud and clear,
For the whole wide world to hear.

Because Wales forever
And here I'll stay
And I'll live here forever
Until my dying day.

Brittany Teague (11)
Pendoylan CW Primary School, Cowbridge

Seasons

Summer is hot, orange and light yellow,
It tastes like a freezing raspberry ripple ice cream,
It sounds like the big blue splashing waves roaring up
                                         onto the seaside shore,
It looks like the ocean with all the amazing sea creatures
                                         swimming through the water,
It smells like candyfloss and chips sailing through the air
                                         from the fairground,
It makes me feel happy and joyful all through the season.

Autumn is crispy brown and dark yellow,
It tastes like cream tea biscuits,
It sounds like bangs coming from gleaming fireworks,
It looks like a crispy golden royal carpet,
It smells like delicious yummy sweets from trick or treating,
It makes me feel all warm and snug.

Winter is plain white, cold and dark,
It tastes like scrumptious Christmas pudding warming up my mouth,
It sounds like sparkling snowflakes gliding gently down to
                                         the icy, wet ground,
It looks like the land of the snow queen because it is a magical land,
It smells like boiling hot soup bubbling in the saucepan,
It makes me feel warm, cold and snug.

Spring is green and white,
It tastes like lamb for Sunday dinner,
It sounds like the *baa* of the baby white lambs
It looks like hundreds of buttercups and daisies,
It smells like the fresh green grass growing in the cool sun,
It makes me feel happy all through each day of the season.

Peta Williams (8)
Pendoylan CW Primary School, Cowbridge

Seasons Poem

Summer is bright and white,
It tastes like a creamy ice cream,
It sounds like a buzzing bee,
It looks like fun floating in the air,
It smells like happiness in the big world,
It makes me feel really, really happy.

Autumn is brown, red and orange,
It tastes like people eating sizzling sausages on Bonfire Night,
It sounds like hundreds of screams on scary Hallowe'en,
It looks like red, green and orange leaves scattering on the dusty floor,
It smells like hot dogs sizzling in the air at a barbecue on Bonfire Night,
It makes me feel warm and cosy.

Winter is sparkly white,
It tastes like soup with warm tea,
It sounds like blobs of very, very cold snow falling all day,
It looks like children playing snowmen,
It smells like people eating hot dogs at Christmas,
It makes me feel happy and joyful.

Jules Orchard-Brown (8)
Pendoylan CW Primary School, Cowbridge

War

War is havoc striking through life,
What is war? A bunch of strife.
People like Hitler, bad and mean,
Kids with guns still in their teens.
Nuclear bombs, missiles and war,
What are these people fighting for?
Families are concerned about their young,
War is not a game, nor is it fun.

Jacob Clutterbuck (11)
Pendoylan CW Primary School, Cowbridge

Funny Poem
(Based on 'Down Behind The Dustbin' by Michael Rosen)

Down behind the dustbin
I met a dog called Sid
He could smell a bone inside
But couldn't lift the lid.

Down behind the dustbin
I met a dog called Ted
Putting his pyjamas on
And going to his bed.

Down behind the dustbin
I met a dog called Pat
He stole a policeman's outfit
And put on his big blue hat.

Down behind the dustbin
I met a dog called Bert
He had a bleeding finger
And it really hurt.

Nathaniel Cannon (7)
Pendoylan CW Primary School, Cowbridge

Pink Piggy Poem

Plump stomach,
Round grotty nose,
Curly tail twitching,
Mucky and hungry,
Got no manners,
Bathes in mud,
Pink curly ears
And makes a noise
Like this *oink!*

Daniel Peters (9)
Pendoylan CW Primary School, Cowbridge

Seasons Poem

Summer is a bright yellow and light blue
It tastes like melting ice lollies and spicy barbecues
It sounds like laughing happily and the calming sea
It looks like the golden sun caring for everyone
It smells like having fun on a summer holiday
It makes me feel like having fun on the best seasons for everyone

Autumn is dark red and crunching brown
It tastes like crispy buttery toast with burning hot beans
It sounds like burning tyres and blue raindrops starting to fall
It looks like a beautiful queen's cloak getting bigger and bigger
It smells like it's a happy year
It makes me feel happy to know I have helped a person at harvest

Winter is snow-white and dark blue
It tastes like a nice warm hot chocolate and warm bubbling soup
It sounds like someone eating a Crunchie chocolate bar
It looks like a plain white cloth covering the whole wide world
It smells like Christmas shopping.
It makes me feel wonderful because it's my birthday season

Spring is an amazing light green and a beautiful blue
It tastes like a juicy apple and a cold drink
It sounds like lambs bleating when a new life begins
It looks like a colourful patch of flowers and a new year beginning
It smells like a kind world beginning
It makes me feel joyful when the sun comes out again.

Brogan Falshaw-Skelly (8)
Pendoylan CW Primary School, Cowbridge

Seasons Poem

Summer is bright yellow and orange,
It tastes like cold vanilla ice cream,
It sounds like hot dazzling sun shining in the sky,
It looks like the hot sun by a fluffy white cloud,
It smells like ice cream sailing the far seas,
It makes my feet hot and sweaty.

Autumn is dark orange and light brown,
It tastes like fireworks shooting off into the bright blue sky,
It sounds like leaves crunching underneath my feet,
It looks like leaves parachuting down from the trees above,
It smells like dead leaves and bare trees in the sky and on the floor,
It makes me feel happy inside.

Winter is dark grey and light blue,
It tastes like warm soup and bread in the frosty cold morning,
It sounds like vicious roaring at you,
It looks like the North Pole where Santa Claus lives,
It smells like cold frost off the trees,
It makes me feel cheerful and free.

Spring is green,
It tastes like summer but not that hot,
It sounds like baby lambs bleating all around,
It looks like baby lambs, buds and leaves,
It smells like calves, lambs and sheep but my favourite is
                              puppies and their silky brown fur,
It makes me feel happy and free!

Ruth David (8)
Pendoylan CW Primary School, Cowbridge

Seasons

Summer is bright yellow and blue,
It tastes like a lovely cold ice cream,
It sounds like a beautiful bird,
It looks like the beautiful golden sun,
It smells like the beautiful smells of the flowers,
It makes me feel happy and fit.

Autumn is the golden leaves in the breeze,
It tastes like the blue and red fireworks and the fire
It sounds like bangs and booms from the fire
It looks like the orange pumpkin
It smells like the hot, yellow fire
It makes me feel happy and cold.

Winter is white and dark grey
It tastes like hot chocolate
It sounds like children playing
It looks like a cold day
It smells of delicious brown turkey
It makes me feel happy and it fills me with joy.

Spring is bright red and green
It tastes like a juicy apple
It sounds like a new baby lamb
it smells like juicy apples
It makes me feel happy and free.

Kieran Moroney (8)
Pendoylan CW Primary School, Cowbridge

Spring

Spring is beautiful pink blossom blowing on the trees,
Spring is white fluffy lambs bleating in the green fields,
Spring is squiggly tadpoles in the blue ponds,
Spring is the delicious chocolate Easter eggs wrapped
                        in rainbow-coloured wrapping paper,
Spring is little chicks wriggling out of their eggs,
Spring is foals cantering with their mums in a green grassy field.

Pippa Loam (8)
Pendoylan CW Primary School, Cowbridge

My Box Of Treasures

(Based on 'Magic Box' by Kit Wright)

I will put in the box . . .
A military shiny green Hummer speeding down the M4 in the sunset,
A Welsh and England rugby team in the Millennium Stadium in Cardiff,
A big, happy, laughing family right beside me when I
                                        am watching television.

I will put in the box . . .
A quality Gamecube up in my little cuddly bedroom,
A nice smell of hay stacked up in the warm barn up the road from me,
A speeding jet as it glides through the night-time sky every week.

I will put in the box . . .
A cuddly bear dressed as a fighter pilot beside me in my comfy bed,
Summertime grass and the farmer's field,
A crashing sea against the beautiful grey seaweedy rock,
A big black monster truck rolling down the street.

James Little (8)
Pendoylan CW Primary School, Cowbridge

Winter

Winter is glorious, winter is fun
Winter is dark with plenty of sparks
The smell of winter is very cold
Plenty of stories waiting to be told
Whiteness spreads all around
You hardly can see anything
As the snow covers the ground
Heaps of snow in your garden
It hardens up everywhere to be found
Blankness swirls from place to place
Snowballs are hitting in your face
Winter is love, it's a bird from up above.

Danielle Murphy (9)
Pendoylan CW Primary School, Cowbridge

Seasons Poem

Summer is bright blue and gold heat
It tastes like lush cold ice cream and a Slush Puppy
It sounds like the wavy blue ocean splashing on the sand
It looks like the sun's reflection on the sea
It makes me feel like making a big golden sandcastle
It smells like salt in the sea.

Autumn is a bright orange dropping from the air and
falling on my head
It tastes like falling red cherries in my mouth
It sounds like crunchy orange leaves when I step on them
It looks like an orange smiley face in the air
It smells like a big juicy melon floating in the sky
It makes me feel like eating toast.

Ethan Hogg (8)
Pendoylan CW Primary School, Cowbridge

Spring

Spring is for the white fluffy lambs gambolling in the field,
Spring is pink blossom hanging on the trees,
Spring is the red roses blooming in the sunshine,
Spring is the big fruit trees, cherries, plums and peaches,
Spring is the little animals crying and making noises,
Spring is the delicious round Easter eggs in all hiding places,
Spring is the big green hills in the distance,
Spring is for when it gets lighter at night,
Spring is the days stretching and getting longer,
Spring is when spiky hedgehogs come out into the soft
warm swaying grass,
Spring is a whole new year.

Lydia McCarthy (8)
Pendoylan CW Primary School, Cowbridge

Funny Poem

Old Mother Hubbard
Went to the cupboard
To fetch her poor dog a bone
But when she got there
The cupboard was bare
And so the poor dog had none

She went to the tailor's
To buy him a coat
But when she came back
He was riding a goat

She went to the Spar
To buy him a bar
But when she came back
He was eating a car

She went to the bar
To buy him a drink
But when she came back
He was eating the sink

She went to the market
To buy him some food
When she came back
He was in a mood.

Libby Mouncher (8)
Pendoylan CW Primary School, Cowbridge

Seasons Poem

Summer is a wild blue
It tastes like mushy meringue and delicious strawberries
and creamy cream,
It sounds like happy people laughing and jumping,
It looks like sunny rays peeping through the cloudy holes,
It smells like slow waves of a swimming pool,
It makes me feel like jumping into a hot sun.

Autumn is a leafy orange and a dark red,
It tastes like warm chicken and leek pie,
It sounds like the spooky howls and screams of the witching
hour at Hallowe'en,
It looks like a whooshing, falling, sparkly, silver star,
It smells like the rough wood burning away the night,
It makes me feel like camping out before the roaring bonfire.

Winter is a crazy black,
It tastes like thick chicken soup,
It sounds like the white snow clattering on the icy roof,
It looks like a white carpet of cold slush spread across the floor,
It smells like the frost from an ice cream,
It makes me feel like throwing smoothed snowballs.

Spring is a silly green and dopey yellow,
It tastes like a salady chicken salad sandwich,
It looks like free dark green jungle with snooping animals too,
It smells like a dark red rose gleaming in the sunlight,
It makes me feel like yummy chocolate Easter eggs
waiting to be eaten.

Anwen Smith (8)
Pendoylan CW Primary School, Cowbridge

Seasons Poem

Summer is scorching hot orange
It tastes like delicious creamy ice cream
It sounds like birds chirping in the trees
It looks like dancing on a hot summer's day
It smells like roses in the bright green grass
It makes me feel like doing sports all through the season.

Autumn is dark brown and light yellow
It tastes like hot potatoes and Hallowe'en
It sounds like a big bright tractor going across a farm
It looks like rich crops growing out of the ground
It smells like autumn breezes in the air
It makes me feel happy and bright every single day.

Winter is cold frosty-white
It tastes like all different types of hot foods
It sounds like mountains cracking then falling
It looks like people skating on icy frozen rivers
It smells like icy cold breaths
It makes me feel like building a snowman.

Spring is dark orange and bright green
It tastes like milk and warm foods
It sounds like lambs and baby animals running around
It looks like sunsets slowly fading away
It smells like Easter eggs cracking in half
It makes me feel like playing all day.

Oliver Bayer (7)
Pendoylan CW Primary School, Cowbridge

Seasons

Summer is bright blazing yellow and bright green
It tastes like cold ice
It sounds like the soft waves in the air
It looks like bright yellow daisies in the fields
It smells like the sweet honey from the honey tree
It makes me feel like being in the Caribbean.

Autumn is brown and dark red
It tastes like soft yellow cheese on toast
It sounds like the leaves rustling in the trees
It looks like the leaves falling off the tree
It smells like the sweet smell of sweets from Hallowe'en
It makes me feel like being in a sweet factory.

Winter is powdery white snow
It tastes like hot cocoa when I come in from the snow
It sounds like the snow pattering on the window
It looks like the big snowdrops falling from the sky
It smells like roast dinner on Christmas Day
It makes me feel happy and joyful.

Spring is bright green colourful leaves
It tastes like the chocolate from the Easter eggs
It sounds like the cows mooing in the field
It looks like the lambs being born
It smells like the flowers in the fields
It makes me feel happy.

Lewis Morgan (8)
Pendoylan CW Primary School, Cowbridge

Seasons

Summer is gold and yellow
It tastes like creamy coleslaw
It sounds like birds cheeping in the morning
It looks like a sunny day in yellow sun
It smells like perfume in the flower
It makes me happy and smiley

Autumn is crunchy nut-brown and golden
It tastes like syrupy cornflakes in a china bowl
It sounds like howling ghosts
It looks scary like a witch
It smells like the smoke from the bonfire
It makes me feel scared

Winter is the glistening white snow
It tastes like hot tomato and lentil soup
It sounds like people singing Christmas carols
It looks like icing on a fruit cake
I feel happy playing in the snow

Spring is purple, yellow, pink and green
It tastes like soft purple grapes
It sounds like foxgloves swinging in the breeze
It looks like a rainbow of flowers
It smells like a flowery perfume
It makes me feel happy in the garden.

Michael Boon (8)
Pendoylan CW Primary School, Cowbridge

My Box Of Treasures

(Based on 'Magic Box' by Kit Wright)

I will put in my brown box . . .
A brightly coloured blue train steaming down the track on
                                                  a sunny morning,
A song thrush singing a beautiful song on the old oak tree
And a rabbit dancing and jumping on the springtime grass.

I will put in my brown box . . .
A chocolate chip cake with blue icing in the kitchen ready to
                                                  be served for dessert,
A fisherman fishing for herring and cod on the splashing blue sea
And a piano playing old and new tunes on a rainy day.

Aaron Parsons (8)
Pendoylan CW Primary School, Cowbridge

Funny Poem

Down behind the dustbin
I met a dog called Sid
He could smell a bone inside
But couldn't lift the lid

Down behind the dustbin
I met a dog called Ted
Putting his pyjamas on
And going to bed

Down behind the dustbin
I met a dog called Pat
He was looking for a big bone
Opened the dustbin and found a rat.

Oliver Lloyd (8)
Pendoylan CW Primary School, Cowbridge

Funny Poem

Jack and Jill went up the hill
To fetch a pail of water
Jack fell down and broke his crown
And Jill came tumbling after

Bob and Bet went up the hill
To fetch a loaf of bread
Bob fell down and broke his crown
And Bet tucked him in bed

Sam and Sue went up the hill
To fetch the dog a bone
Sam fell down and broke his crown
And Sue was on the phone.

Joshua Matthews (7)
Pendoylan CW Primary School, Cowbridge

Football

This is a really beautiful game,
People think rugby is the same.
Football is full of passion and pride,
And when you're a fan it can jolt you inside.
Scoring goals is how you win,
If you hit the post your head starts to spin.
Scoring a free kick is a work of art,
And wearing your socks up to your knees
                    will make you look the part.
Ninety minutes is the end of the game,
When the whistle blows you'll never feel the same.

James Williams (10)
Pendoylan CW Primary School, Cowbridge

It's A Funny Thing But . . .

I've seen a
Black, swinging gorilla
And a
Golden, roaring lion
But I've never seen a
Red, flying dog.

I've seen a
Brown, scampering mouse
And a
Silver, swimming fish
But I've never seen a
Turquoise, flying sheep.

Kyle Reid (8)
Penybont Primary School, Bridgend

It's A Funny Thing But . . .

I've seen a
Brown, scampering hedgehog
And a
Dark, crimson, fire-breathing dragon
But I've never seen a
Pink, cool dinosaur.

I've seen a
Brown, laughing hyena
And a
Black, creepy, crawling spider
But I've never seen a
Blue, flying, fluffy rhino.

Benjamin Cruickshank (8)
Penybont Primary School, Bridgend

It's A Funny Thing But . . .

I've seen a
Black and white zebra
And a
Grey, splashing dolphin,
But I've never seen an
Orange, flying dog.

I've seen a
Brown, swinging monkey
And a
Green, slithering crocodile
But I've never seen a
Yellow, skipping whale.

Hannah Evans (8)
Penybont Primary School, Bridgend

The Castle Ghost

The castle ghost
Glides along the dark dungeons
Like a slithering, silver outline.
He floats through the lord's chamber
Like a shivering, silver eagle.

The castle ghost
Hovers up the spiral staircase
Like a pale cloud.
He swoops above the empty moat
Like white snow.

The dreadful castle ghost.

Ryan Pickford (8)
Penybont Primary School, Bridgend

The Castle Ghost

The castle ghost
Flies along the stone battlements
Like a snowy owl.
He glides through the dark dungeons
Like a silver, slithering snake.

The castle ghost
Swoops up the tall keep
Like a silver dragon.
He darts between the narrow arrow slits
Like a sharp arrow.

The watchful castle ghost.

Geraint Lang (8)
Penybont Primary School, Bridgend

Death

Death is black.
It smells like poisonous gases.
The taste of something cold and bitter.
Sounding of people wailing.
The feel of sharp spikes piercing.
Death lives at the end of your life.

Luke Williams (10)
Penybont Primary School, Bridgend

Disease

Disease is green.
It smells like putrefying bodies.
Tastes like sewage.
The sound of sadness and beloved ones crying,
Feeling full of pain and sorrow.
It lives deep in your body.

Jack Mantell (10)
Penybont Primary School, Bridgend

Animal Alliteration

Drunken donkeys drawing dreadfully,
Sunburned swans swimming in a swamp,
Five fat fish falling,
Tamed tigers taking tests,
Lemon lions licking lollies,
Jewelled jaguars juggling jaffas,
Mean monkeys making mint sauce.

Tyler Walsh (8)
Penybont Primary School, Bridgend

Animal Alliteration

Angry aardvarks adding ants,
Busy beavers breaking boulders,
Crazy crocodiles cracking cauliflowers,
Silly snakes smoking cigarettes,
Drunken donkeys driving dynamite,
Mad monkeys mopping mats,
Lazy lobsters laying lynxes.

Sam Townend (8)
Penybont Primary School, Bridgend

Old Age

Old age is silver.
It smells of ancient, long hair.
It tastes of fermenting apples on trees
And sounds like chilly drips in a dark dungeon.
It feels like the crooked ending to a journey.
Old age lives even with the newest born baby.

Owen Smith (10)
Penybont Primary School, Bridgend

2060, Venus Orbit

2060,
A new adventure in space begins . . .
Destination: Venus.
A hot and deadly volcanic world,
Shimmering amber, sphere of light
Appears in my misty, glass window,
Closer, as my orbit begins.
A trickle of sweat running down my neck
As burning fear overcomes me,
My heart pounding like a drum.
Beneath my rocket,
A world of erupting volcanoes with burning lava spitting,
Hits my eyes.
Control panel lights
Suddenly flashing red . . .
Danger!
The scorching acid planet
Swallowing my spaceship whole,
Powerfully pulling at my helpless, melting craft.
A new adventure in space ends . . .
2060.

**Joshua James, Molly Powles, Jamie Smith, Imogen Stewart,
Kirsty Bradley & Paisley Thompson-Bailey (9)**
Penybont Primary School, Bridgend

Disappointment

Disappointment is blue.
It smells like wet dirt mouldering.
It tastes like grime and dust.
The sounds are like boulders falling from cliffs
And crashing together.
It feels sharp, ice and cold.
Disappointment lives in the heart of a cold, dark, gloomy cave.

Heather Johnston (10)
Penybont Primary School, Bridgend

Contrasts

Earth, a friendly planet,
Venus, a hostile, barren land.
Earth, a fertile, blue and green sphere,
Venus, sandy, dry and deadly.
Earth, surrounded by swirling, white candyfloss clouds,
Venus with clouds of hungry acid.
Earth, beauty in sea, plants and life,
Venus, danger in burning, orange, volcanic ash.
Earth, a safe, water-filled balloon,
Venus, a ball of dying flames.
Earth, fresh, bright and lively,
Venus, destructive, evaporative and crushing.
Earth, our respected home planet,
Venus . . . we are not quite sure.

**Jamie-Leigh Morgan, Chelsee Davies, Lloyd Griffiths,
Ashley Dobbs, Kate Evans & Lucy Richards (9)**
Penybont Primary School, Bridgend

Fearful Times On A Magic Carpet

I wanted to
Sail over the rainforest
Hide on the branches
Feel the tickle of leaves rub gently
I wanted to sit there
Watching all day
But the carpet took me to school!

I wanted to
Drift over Disneyland
Watch the lovely fireworks
Crash in the air
See the bright colours
Zoom across the sky
And yellow stars fall
I wanted to sit there all day watching
But the carpet took me to school!

Jordan Louise Barclay (9)
Penyrenglyn Primary School, Treherbert

Fearful Times On A Magic Carpet

I wanted to
Fly to Atlantis,
See the peaceful Atlantians,
Explore their wrecked city,
I wanted to feel adventurous
But the carpet took me to school!

I wanted to
Float to the cheesy moon,
Taste the yellow cheese,
See an alien that's really cool,
I wanted to feel like an astronaut
But the carpet took me to school!

I wanted to
Glide to the steamy rainforest,
To bounce on the soft, green canopy,
And slide down the bubbling waterfall,
I wanted to feel like Tarzan
But the carpet took me to school!

Beth Moulsdale (9)
Penyrenglyn Primary School, Treherbert

Wilderness

(Based on 'Hatchet' by Gary Paulsen)

On the horizon golden, glorious sun shines above the forest.
Far out in the lake lives a big, scary fish.
In the shallows huge, black bears are drinking fresh water.
Outside the shelter a spiky porcupine prepares to shoot.
High in the sky a beautiful bald eagle swoops.
Somewhere in the distance grey wolves howl at the moon.
In the branches breathtaking butterflies flutter.

Hanna Wakeford (11)
Penyrenglyn Primary School, Treherbert

Fearful Times On A Magic Carpet

I wanted to
Glide over the tropical rainforest
To see the monkey swaying from tree to tree
Watch the tiger pounce on its prey
I wanted to feel free
But the carpet took me to school.

I wanted to
Zoom into the galaxy
Speak to aliens from different planets
Survive where there is no air
I wanted to experience Mars
But the carpet took me to school.

It's not fair
I wanted to stay up in the air
But the carpet took me to school!

Alexander Jenkins (9)
Penyrenglyn Primary School, Treherbert

I Am What I Consume

Oh yes
Spicy, delicious chicken biryani
With white, fluffy rice,
A spicy, hot dish
With crunchy, fragile poppadoms.
I am what I consume.

Nathan Williams (11)
Penyrenglyn Primary School, Treherbert

Fearful Times On A Magic Carpet

I wanted to -
Sway over the Mediterranean Sea
See the dolphins jumping and splashing
Watch the waves crashing
I wanted to feel free
But the carpet took me to school.

I wanted to -
Flutter over the tropical rainforest
Feel the spiky branches on the treetops
Listen to the tigers and lions roaring
I wanted to roar with them
But the carpet took me to school.

I wanted to -
Hover over Atlantis
See the Atlantians doing their rain dance
Listen and sing along with them
I wanted to feel as if I was one of them
But the carpet took me to school.

Jordan Haskins (9)
Penyrenglyn Primary School, Treherbert

I Am What I Consume

Oh yes
Long, messy, delicious Bolognese,
With a juicy, meaty sauce,
A tasty, beefy chunk of Bolognese
On a bed of long, tangled spaghetti.

Danielle Morgan (11)
Penyrenglyn Primary School, Treherbert

Fearful Times On A Magic Carpet

I wanted to
Swoop to Egypt,
See the dusty pyramids,
Touch the sparkling statues,
I wanted to feel free
But the carpet took me to school!

I wanted to
Dive under the sea,
Glide along with the dolphins,
See them swim fast,
I wanted to feel fantastic
But the carpet took me to school!

I wanted to
Dash to Disneyland,
See Mickey Mouse,
Have a photo with him,
I wanted to stay and play
But the carpet took me to school!

Samantha Rees (9)
Penyrenglyn Primary School, Treherbert

Cold Wind

I can freeze your tingling fingers and your hot toes,
Help Jack Frost make your curved nose numb,
My chilling breath will blow you off your feet.
But I can't melt your ice-cold ice cream in the summer sun
Or make the cold, children sweat.

Laurie Edwards (10)
Penyrenglyn Primary School, Treherbert

Fearful Times On A Magic Carpet

I wanted to . . .
Fly over the mountains,
Land on the tops.
Watch the birds glide,
I wanted to feel free
But the carpet took me to school!

Michael Hill (9)
Penyrenglyn Primary School, Treherbert

Seasons

Spring
In the lovely spring,
When animals have babies,
The flowers grow tall.

Summer
When it is summer,
The people play at the beach,
And play in the sea.

Autumn
In the cold autumn
When the leaves fall off the trees
They land on the ground.

Winter
In the cold winter
The people make tall snowmen
And play snowball fights.

Sophie Bird (8)
Radyr Primary School, Cardiff

Super Stackpole

Stackpole, lovely beaches,
Beautiful birds and insects.
Educational and interesting,
Canoeing fabulous,
Biking too.
I feel cosy and warm
As I walk along the coast.
I see tremendous wildlife.
Along the coast I hear birds singing,
The sunrays making flowers bloom,
Owned by National Trust's amazing eco code.
I can smell all the violets,
Mystical creatures crawling.
The sea makes me happy, crashing on rocks.
The buzzing of bees collecting honey.
As I climb I am so joyful.
Finding crabs in rock pools is superb.
Peaceful and calm is Stackpole.

Olivia Kendall (10)
Radyr Primary School, Cardiff

Dragon

Your triangular wings flutter and flap
Your breath is as hot as steam
Red, orange and yellow flames wrap around you
Up in the sky where you like to be.
As your claws like steel
As sharp as blades
Stretch out towards your prey
Back to your cave you fly.

Lucy Fuszard (8)
Radyr Primary School, Cardiff

Winter Snow

Sparkling snow in the winter breeze,
Lands on your nose and makes you sneeze.
Snow,
A white blanket on the lawn,
Starts at the first hour of day,
Jumping in the snow of light,
Excited from day to night,
Cold snow lying down.

Melting ice everywhere,
Snowdrifts,
In the white, fluffy clouds,
Twisting and turning and spinning around,
Landing on the soft ground,
Back to the cold breeze of winter
And then it comes back again next year.

Hannah Dykes (8)
Radyr Primary School, Cardiff

Bengal Tiger Of Asia

India, the country of the Bengal tiger,
The species that deserves the name 'rare',
Hunting this animal is a desire of evil.
Who would dare do such a thing?
Whoever does it must be out of their minds,
After all, they must be worth more when they're alive.
You must get more money from the tourists
Than from selling their meat or fur
And so it can be said they're nicer alive than dead.

Henry Holms (8)
Radyr Primary School, Cardiff

Winter

Flowing in the winter breeze,
Watch you don't catch a cold
And cough and sneeze.
The town will freeze from head to toe,
Cars will go under the snow for a while
And you will never know!

The ice will melt suddenly
And there will be no snow
And all that will be left
Is a winter flow
That will soon go
And leave south
With the winter snow.

For the last time the trees will howl and blow
And we can't believe that frosty old winter
Has gone and will be no more.

Bradley Bennett (8)
Radyr Primary School, Cardiff

Mystery Animal

Mystery animal can swim in the sea,
Mystery animal can see inside her shell,
Mystery animal can put her arms and legs in her shell,
Mystery animal is very slow,
Mystery animal can walk on land as well,
Mystery animal is an amphibian,
Mystery animal lays her eggs in the sand.
Can you guess who she is?

Mystery animal, she is Turtle!

Daniel Lâm Wan (8)
Radyr Primary School, Cardiff

Mystical Nature

We have a secret way
Of surviving through the day
Creeping up walls
In mysterious ways.
They ruined our land
Everything was falling through our hands.
We took revenge, taking over mankind.
We are not the strongest . . . yet.

We are still here fighting to stay
Making friends every new day.
We make flowers bloom
And insects play.
Sometimes we have hurt
But there is a reason
To stay every season.
Nature is good, not bad
So there's no need to be sad.
Nature is mystical.

Hannah Jayne Williams (8)
Radyr Primary School, Cardiff

All The Stars

All the stars come out at night,
Shimmering,
Shining,
All so bright,
They paint the sky full of light.

When morning comes,
They die away,
So come out, sun,
It's time to play.

Isabella Strinati (8)
Radyr Primary School, Cardiff

Magical India

India,
The hot, hot country,
In big, big Asia
With all of the cool, cool saris
And the beautiful Taj Mahal.

The dark, dark forest
With the wild, wild tiger.
His black and orange stripes
Hiding in the trees.

With the lovely, lovely Indian food
And the fantastic Indian sweets.
All the grey, grey elephants
Having a muddy, muddy bath
In the bright, bright sunlight.

Jacob Watkins (8)
Radyr Primary School, Cardiff

I Am A Planet

I am a planet
The second planet in space
I am clothed in blue and white
I am a secret bride
I am veiled with mist and cloud
I am the hottest planet in the solar system
I spin slowly.

I am the planet of mystery
My deadly atmosphere poisons people
I look calm but I can be angry
Sending my messenger lightning.
I am the goddess of love, peace and joy
I am Venus, the goddess of love
And dangerous beauty.

Sanvitti Bengeri (9)
Radyr Primary School, Cardiff

In The Jungle

Walking through the jungle,
Looking for pink and white birds,
Animals' eyes spying on me,
I see the birds I'm looking for,
Sipping the crystal-clear water near me.

I take a precarious picture,
As the water turns brown,
And the birds start flapping and squawking,
I leave to see another animal.

Walking through jungle,
Look for scaly, spiral snakes,
I was weary when I approached them,
So I took a picture . . .

And I ran!

Ffion Brown (8)
Radyr Primary School, Cardiff

A Grey Cloud

One grey cloud turns over a tree
It strikes with thunder
And the tree falls on me.
And now I am a spirit
A spirit from a tree
I am in Heaven
Lots of hard, old bodies
Hanging over me.
I am shivering like thunder
Over a tree
And now I am feeling a tree
Falling on me.
I am stiff, stiff as a tree
I feel lonely
With my life in a tree.
I have no friends to comfort me.

Kristy Philipps (8)
Radyr Primary School, Cardiff

Dragon

I am a dragon swimming through boiling water
I am a dragon searching for everlasting torture
I am a dragon going to bed
I am a dragon with an aching head.

I live with ghosts chained to posts
I live with spirits
They howl like crickets
I live with bats, they cry like cats.

I am a dragon failing in the flood
I am a dragon wearing a red, scaly hood.

I am an old dragon
I'm in a grave
My cries of sorrow
Fill the cave
My tears of sadness
Are a waterfall of badness.

Lois Leach (9)
Radyr Primary School, Cardiff

Chelsea, Chelsea!

Chelsea, Chelsea are the best
Beats Wenger's Arsenal side, no mess.
Winning all trophies because they're immense.

Now it's the end of the season,
Chelsea have no games to play
So I have to wait till next season
To win the rest.

It's the new season now,
More trophies to win
To bring to Stamford bridge
And become champions.

Steffan Gray-Davies (8)
Radyr Primary School, Cardiff

Speeding Cars, Bumpy Trucks And Wobbly Bikes

Speeding cars down the motorway
Speeding cars down the road
Speeding cars going everywhere
Speeding cars don't take a load.

Bumpy trucks going crazy
Bumpy trucks going mad
Who do you think is driving it?
Maybe it could be your dad.

Wobbly bikes going down the road
Wobbly bikes going down the street
Wobbly bikes going down the mountain
Wobbly bikes are very neat.

William Sewell (8)
Radyr Primary School, Cardiff

Best Friends

Best friends are big friends
They have sleepovers and makeovers
Like all friends do.
I wonder what it would be like
If nobody had friends?
Think of it -
No birthdays and no good days,
No playing, no laughing,
Nothing like that.
So have a best friend
That you can share secrets with
And dare with.
Have a best friend just like me.

Jennifer Davies (8)
Radyr Primary School, Cardiff

Stackpole

Stackpole
On the Pembroke coast
The bright, blue sea
Sparkling in the sun
Exploring the dark, little caves
Making sculptures in the sand
All the seabirds zooming around
Hiding from seagulls
All the little insects
Hovering above our heads
Watching coots and moorhen
Swimming in the lake
Feeling excited but tired
Listening to crashing waves
Smelling lovely flowers.
We're here to learn about nature.

David Bernard (10)
Radyr Primary School, Cardiff

Stackpole Poem

I'm at Stackpole walking on the coast
I feel the cold wind in my face
I can hear the waves crashing on the rocks
Canoeing, abseiling, cycling
Amazing birds flying above my head
They're zooming everywhere
Bees buzzing, ants crawling, flies flying
The sun beaming down on the ground
All flowers blooming
I can smell the flowers and trees
You can catch crabs in the rock pools
We came to learn about nature.
Stackpole.

Max Gilmore (10)
Radyr Primary School, Cardiff

Stackpole

Stackpole
Around me the beautiful lakes and woods
The smell of fresh air
Small amount of noise
Going canoeing, abseiling, rock climbing
I'm excited
Having the best of fun
Scurrying off, talking, going to the next activity
Coming back for lunch, superb food
Rain splashing down now
Trekking out again in the rain
Cycling, very wet
I feel adventurous
But it won't last forever
Make the most of it
While you still can
Have a laugh
At Stackpole.

Stephanie Taylor (10)
Radyr Primary School, Cardiff

Dragon

Scales sparkle like stars in the night.
Breathing your fire, it's your secret light.
Sleeping and dreaming deep in a cave.
Stretching your wings,
You whiz through the air,
Roaring as you fly around.
Your magical wings
Help you again.
Dragons are mystical creatures, I can tell.

Lucy Jawad (8)
Radyr Primary School, Cardiff

Stackpole

Stackpole is around the corner,
Excitement is flowing through my veins,
Sea, sand, sun, what more could you want?
The peaceful woods make Stackpole more brilliant.

In the canoe,
I flow across the lake with ease,
The zooming feeling is still inside me,
I buzz just thinking about it.

Trying to find a crack to step in,
Rock climbing feels wonderful,
Abseiling back to the ground,
I feel like I'm flying above the people below.

Biking around the peaceful, silent woods,
Going through the puddles and rivers is great fun,
All the mud getting stuck in my wheels,
My equipment getting covered in slushy mud.

Stackpole is fantastic,
In every single way,
The wonderful nature,
I wish I could stay forever!

Amy O'Neill (10)
Radyr Primary School, Cardiff

Animals Are Friends

African animals roaming the land
Lions prowling round for food
Kangaroos hopping, ready to whip any poachers that come
If anything happened the rhino would charge
That's why all animals are friends
Like we should be . . . always.

Rachel Jones (8)
Radyr Primary School, Cardiff

Stackpole

A great eco centre,
For outdoor education,
Fun and learning.
The big, blue sea,
The shimmering sand,
The dark caves
And the great wildlife sounds.

Going canoeing in the minibus,
We'll get soaked.
Rock climbing, abseiling,
All great fun.
Cycling and orienteering
Great fun too.
All the activities are great fun.

All the crabs, big and small
Can we catch them all?
Starfish so small or so big,
Orangey-yellow with lots of little bumps.
Prawns and shrimps
So very fast.
All swimming in the tank in crab corner.

Kathryn Rees (9)
Radyr Primary School, Cardiff

Stackpole

S uper Stackpole simply sunny
T remendous time thinking
A crobatic abseiling
C rab catching
K itchen knapsack
P retty ponds
O rienteering over obstacles
L ooking at lily pads
E ating everything edible.

Will Hutton (10)
Radyr Primary School, Cardiff

Aberdeen

I am in Aberdeen
Sitting on the golden sand
On the beach
It feels tremendous
The ice cream tastes delicious
So quiet and peaceful
The waves so calm
Seagulls flying in the sky
More people arriving
A family going to swim in the sea
Enjoying every moment
I start to walk around
Some children making sandcastles
Some splashing water
The sand is wet
Children are coming to get it
Everyone going in their car
Ready to go home.

Brinda Ahya (9)
Radyr Primary School, Cardiff

Friends

Everyone says you need friends
That are careful, kind and funny.
Everyone says you need friends
With names just like Honey.

Everyone says you need friends
That are kind to people's pets.
Everyone says you need friends
That ride a super-fast jet.

Everyone says you need friends
That go with you to the pool.
Everyone says you need friends
That are completely *cool!*

Rebecca Alsept (11)
Radyr Primary School, Cardiff

My Dream World

In my dream world,
The sun is always shining.
The sky is clear and blue,
Everyone is welcome, even you!

In my dream world,
The beaches are clear and sandy
And the forests are made of candy.

In my dream world,
Everything is peaceful and quiet
(But not when my brother comes to visit!)

In my dream world,
There are palm trees
And all-night parties.

Then I open my eyes
And my dream world is gone.

Elin Gronow (11)
Radyr Primary School, Cardiff

Amazing Stackpole

Wonderful Stackpole is filled with happiness,
I hear beautiful robins singing in the sky,
I see the Pembrokeshire coastline gently swimming with waves,
I smell the fresh and peaceful breeze,
I am here to study the wildlife and excellent nature,
I do lots of activities in the nice, bright sun,
I feel glorious, excited and brilliant,
I am filled with perfectness and harmony.

The flowers are super and they smell great,
Stackpole is *amazing!*

Sahithya Balachandran (10)
Radyr Primary School, Cardiff

In The Playground

They're arguing in the playground, Miss,
They said it was a goal,
It went ten metres wide, Miss,
And broke poor Peter's nose!

I am getting bullied, Miss,
They're leaving me out of their game.
They are playing armies, Miss,
And I've got a really good aim!

They're fighting over girls, Miss,
They all fancy Emma Drew,
There are much better ones than her, Miss,
Not many, but there are a few!

Shut up, shut up, shut up, kids,
Stop telltaling to me.
You're getting worse and worse, kids,
Especially you three!

Matthew Smith (11)
Radyr Primary School, Cardiff

Stackpole

Beautiful lakes
Perfect and peaceful
Zooming birds
Looking at the map
Fragrant flowers
Flying in the water
Go up the sloppy
Climbing walls.

Jared Donnelly (10)
Radyr Primary School, Cardiff

Stackpole

I am in Stackpole
I see beautiful birds in trees
I can hear them tweeting
I feel the wind
I am walking by the trees and lakes
I'm with my group
Walking past the lakes with herons hovering
Everyone is having a brilliant time
There is a peaceful sound of buzzing bees
We look at the tremendous sights
A brilliant bird and habitat
Big, blooming skies
Looking at the environment
Fantastic times.

Elizabeth Lyle (10)
Radyr Primary School, Cardiff

Stackpole

By the coastline in Broad Haven Bay,
I see birds screeching and squawking,
I smell the tangy smell of salt,
I feel the waves crashing against the rocks,
I feel happy and excited.
I'm here for the activities
And to learn about the environment.
My group stares around in awe,
I get closer to the cliff
And closer.
I peer down,
I see birds,
They hover about in the air.
Finally I leave.

Georges Nolan (10)
Radyr Primary School, Cardiff

Stackpole

I am in the Stackpole camp
Having a brill time
Playing games with my friends
I see my friends playing Top T
And having a good time.

We all go down for dinner
What's that lovely smell?
I think it's jacket potato.
The jacket potato is lovely
So is the strawberries and ice cream.

We all go upstairs
Then come back.
We all have some sweets
And most gobbled them down.
Once we'd finished we went to bed.

When I woke up
I said, 'Ow, my aching head.'

Daniel Hallett (10)
Radyr Primary School, Cardiff

Stackpole

The peaceful ocean that lies ahead of Stackpole,
Motionless birds soaring through the sky,
Mystical sights bloom in front of me,
Studying the coast of Stackpole.
The wind hovers around me,
Nature noises combine together,
Wonderful creatures gather up,
Buzzing bees around us.
Fantastic, motionless beaches,
Canoe, climb, cycle,
Putting my equipment on
As I discover the adventures of Stackpole.

Jade Chan (10)
Radyr Primary School, Cardiff

Stackpole

I'm going to Stackpole,
But I'm sure to miss my parents.
The class is noisy,
The are excited like me.
At the moment we are stuck in a coach.
The air is stale and stuffy,
But we will soon be breathing fresh air
In Pembrokeshire Nature Reserve.
I'm glad to be off the coach,
We are finding out our rooms.
My room is Puffins Burrow,
I share it with Georges and William.
I sleep on the top-right bunk bed.
We have gone down for lunch,
A sandwich with a chocolate muffin for dessert.
Delicious.
Now we are going exploring.
I've got on my walking boots,
Have you?
Let's do some activities.
Biking is great fun,
I am lost doing orienteering.
Canoeing can get you wet.
A red-eyed crab for rock pooling.
Rock climbing rocks.
You can't beat sand sculpting.
The best 5 days of my life.

Dhyanesh Patel (10)
Radyr Primary School, Cardiff

Breakfast

It's chaos at breakfast,
Everything's a mess.
Food is flying everywhere,
On mum's best dress.

My sister wants some sausages,
My brother wants some cheese.
Dad just wants some quiet,
So he can pay his fees.

My mum is late for a meeting,
I am late for school.
But with my breakfast on my face,
I will look like a fool.

The dog is on the table,
My sister's making a noise.
The kitchen floor is covered,
With my little brother's toys.

But once it's all over,
It isn't that bad.
Everything is peaceful,
Except for an angry dad.

Tom Hutchinson (11)
Radyr Primary School, Cardiff

Stackpole

Past the old, oak tree,
Overlooking the blue sea,
Is Stackpole Centre.

There's weeks full of fun,
An adventure each day,
Don't want to come home.

Lots of surprises,
It's like eating a sandwich
In a Stackpole lunch.

Harriet Dykes
Radyr Primary School, Cardiff

My Dream

I dream I'm in Portugal,
A quite beautiful island,
And out of nowhere this shimmering creature came,
With a colourful body, two golden legs,
Sitting in a tree trying to rest.
One little baby crying for food,
A big daddy fishing in the stream, he caught a fish,
Takes it back to mother and baby
Who are sitting in the nest hungry.
Soon the nest will fall apart and with a few helping hands
And mud and twigs
A happy family will have a nest.

Guess yet?

Yes, it's a tropical bird!

Jessica Alice Evans (9)
Radyr Primary School, Cardiff

Cardiff Blues

C ardiff Blues are always winning.
A ll of them winning and winning.
R ight and wrong, everyone's working hard.
D angerous and deadly, breaking through defenders.
I t looks great, it's Cardiff Blues.
F ar and near, everyone's losing to them.
F lying up the league table.

B lue and black always win.
L ast match was 68 to 3, how can they do it?
U nbelievable speed, never stopping.
E nd of pitch, a spectacular try.
S unday's evening never fails for the Blues.

James Cargill (9)
Radyr Primary School, Cardiff

Hell Is Now Full

Hell is now full,
There is just no more room,
We don't know where to put people,
Who have killed their Aunt Bloom.

Hell is now full,
There's just nothing left to do,
We have tried absolutely everything,
There is not even room in the loo.

Hell is now full,
We told you a minute ago,
'Yes, but why?' they ask
Because you're so bad, you just don't know.

Hell is now full,
My head is going to burst!
But I think my eyes and ears,
Are definitely going to go first.

'Okay, okay, okay,' I say,
I'll try and make some room now,
Just do me a favour and go around Earth,
To tell people, *think before you do bad things from now.*

Alex Alsept (11)
Radyr Primary School, Cardiff

There's More To Pizza Hut

There's more to Pizza Hut
Than meets the eye.
Chicken curry, French fries
With purple toppings
That look like bird droppings.

With Coke that smells of smoke
'Pizza Hut,' the children shout.
But soon they'll be chanting
'Pizza Hut, let's get out!'

Zoë M Delport (9)
Radyr Primary School, Cardiff

Who Am I?

I swim in the sea,
Fluttering through the waves,
Making lots of noise,
Eating away.

> My colour is grey
> And I've got a sharp spike,
> I'm going through the seaweed,
> Making loads of fright.

Swimming very fast,
Scaring all the fishes,
Then going out of sight.

> Zooming through the sea,
> I am really free.

Who am I?

> *A shark!*

Ryan Dando (9)
Radyr Primary School, Cardiff

Body Explorers

Climbing up your snotty nose,
Checking you can breathe,
Rubbing sandpaper on your tongue,
To roughen it up ready for food,
Sliding down your slippery spine,
Making sure everything's fine,
Jumping up and down upon your heart,
Tobogganing down your guts in a cart,
Pumping blood all around you,
What would you do without us?

Megan Mary Thomas (9)
Radyr Primary School, Cardiff

What Am I?

Whizzing through the sky
Landing on the ground
Pecking all the worms
Out of the ground.

Nesting in a tree
Collecting twigs
Having babies in a lovely tree.

Kicking all the leaves
Stamping on the ground
Meeting others all around.

When it gets cold fly away
Come back on a sunny day.

What am I?

Bird!

Heather Morgan (9)
Radyr Primary School, Cardiff

Stackpole

S tackpole is so super
T aking care of nature
A bseiling is so cool
C anoeing, cycling and many more
K ittiwakes call
P eople having fun
O utside on an adventure
L earning more and more
E ating everything.

Perry Rowlands (10)
Radyr Primary School, Cardiff

The Troll And The Pound

There was a troll
who went for a stroll
he climbed up a tree
to eat a pea.

Then he fell to the ground
and found a pound
he was so excited
he fell over a cat.

And sat on a mat
he patted the cat
and he put on a hat
the hat was thrilled.

So the troll paid his bills
he killed a snail
and he went all pale.

He swallowed a fly
and he started to cry
because he was going to die.

Ben Hardie (8)
Radyr Primary School, Cardiff

Patrick Vieira

Patrick, Patrick,
Scores a hat-trick
The ball that he snatches,
Wins all the matches,
When he gets flying,
The other team starts crying.

He is the man,
Sticking to the plan,
I am his biggest fan
And so is my mate Dan!

Robert Liguz (8)
Radyr Primary School, Cardiff

Stackpole/Pembroke

S tackpole, simply super school
T remendously terrific time
A bseiling away about April
C anoeing can come courageous
K itchen, ketchup, kettle
P yjamas, pale people
O vercoat over-big
L ovely, liking Labradors
E veryone enjoys education.

P embrokeshire
E verybody enjoys education
M others make me
B rothers buy bread
R eady, rumbling road
O ver-big orchid
K ing kites
E veryone enjoys everywhere.

Alex Brown (10)
Radyr Primary School, Cardiff

What Am I?

Silent stalker,
Quick walker,
Best camouflager.

My hobbies are growling
And best of all prowling.

I look at the flowers flowering
As I start my prowling.

What am I?
    A tiger!

Adam Morris (9)
Radyr Primary School, Cardiff

Brilliant Stackpole

Stackpole, too many words to say,
Perfect beds to sleep in,
I'm here to have a fantastic time,
The birds swoosh in the sky,
You feel magical, that's how special they are,
Activities are amazing, most inspiring,
The smell is sweet and lush,
Flowers bloom in your face.

Outstanding weather just for you,
Rivers, lakes, canoeing, abseiling,
Have a tremendous time,
I hear so many peaceful things,
And feel the air and green things around,
People are so friendly,
Spreading good information,
So caring for this world,
Brings friends and families,
Smooth and rough feelings,
So see what you think.

Charlotte Smith (9)
Radyr Primary School, Cardiff

Magic Stars

Some stars are magic,
They toss in the sky with special dust,
As their spikes dazzle from their shine,
Roaming the sky,
Swirling and zooming away!

Many stars are like diamonds,
About the sky the stars twinkle,
Glowing everywhere,
In the sky they can't see where they're going,
Curling up to go to sleep.

Miriam Smith (8)
Radyr Primary School, Cardiff

Stackpole

I am in Stackpole,
I smell the flowers along the coastline,
I feel peaceful and excited,
I'm here to see all the birds,
Canoeing, cycling and coastal walks,
I see the water splashing beside me,
I hear the buzzing of the bees,
Also I see the birds soaring around me,
A superb view to see,
Skylark, chough, herring gull,
Swooping towards me,
I see the cliff tops,
I see some rope,
I see some people,
I'm ready to climb.

Katie Griffiths (10)
Radyr Primary School, Cardiff

Stackpole

Stackpole, a warm, welcoming place
The sea, the air, the birds, the breeze
Buzzing with excitement, just can't wait
Enjoy myself and have a great time
Canoe, cycle, climb
Climbing steadily up the wall and over
Delicious, the best food ever, honest
Cosy and warm, absolutely fabulous
Wonderful, really cool
Nice, they're really friendly
Comfy and soft, soft and comfy
Fast, hard to find
Brilliant time, one of a kind.

Daniel Perry (10)
Radyr Primary School, Cardiff

Stackpole

I am at Stackpole
I am here for one reason - enjoyment
I've seen the lovely, bright, warm sea
I feel happy, can't wait for tomorrow
Canoeing is amazing
Biking is brilliant
So is rock climbing
The food, smack on
It's a lovely place
Accommodation perfect
So is everything
I am at Stackpole
I am here for one reason - enjoyment
I have done
It is the right place for me.

Elliot Jones (10)
Radyr Primary School, Cardiff

London

I like London, it is great
Except for some people who are so rude
The busy nights are so noisy
I feel like there's no privacy
The toy shop in London is huge
One of the best to you
Why not go to the London Eye?
A lovely sight, so, so high
A lot of flats, around 16 floors
So big, take you a long time to walk
A brilliant place to go
Why not visit all the museums I know?
Shop in the centre all day
You won't get bored at all
The bad thing is you have to go on a 2½ hour ride back to home.

Gary Lee (10)
Radyr Primary School, Cardiff

I Don't Like My Shoes

I don't like my shoes
they're black and grey.

I don't like my shoes
they feel very stiff.

I don't like my shoes
they're hard to run in.

I don't like my shoes
they're not good at football.

I don't like my shoes
they smell funny.

*I don't like my shoes
they're new!*

Joe Crossley-Lewis (8)
Radyr Primary School, Cardiff

Dolly The Dolphin

Dolly the dolphin comes out to play
With her friends every day
Jumping out to say,
'Come on, everyone, come out and play.'
At the end of the day
Dolly the dolphin says, 'Hey!
I will be back another day.'
That is the story of Dolly the dolphin
Who likes jumping, playing and calling for games.
Even when she is sad she likes it all the same.
So as the happy Dolly swims along
We all go and sing a happy song.

Hannah May Williams (8)
Radyr Primary School, Cardiff

Who Is It?

I'm in the sparkling sea
Swimming with the fish
And then a magical creature
Jumps out of the water
Its shimmering tail sparkles
In the sunlight
With long, blonde hair.
Who is it?

It's a mermaid!

Briony Powell (9)
Radyr Primary School, Cardiff

Poetry

Happy days are there,
Playing around with friends.
Just games everywhere.

Stackpole's very great fun,
Cycling is good in the woods,
Along in the sun.

It's great, you should come,
There's lots to do there
And fun everywhere.

Susanna Smith (9)
Radyr Primary School, Cardiff

The Private Badger

His face is black and white
And he sleeps all day and gets up at night.
The reason he sleeps all day
Is because he keeps out of danger's way.
He lives in a sett under the ground
And at night he searches for food.

Jack Hooper (9)
Radyr Primary School, Cardiff

Yu-Gi-Oh

Yu-gi-oh, you're my game,
All the others
Are so lame.

Yu-gi-oh rocks,
Pokemon stinks
Of old, smelly socks.

Yu-gi-oh's great
And Pokemon's
The one to hate.

Taylor Sumers (9)
Radyr Primary School, Cardiff

Daffodils

Daffodils, so beautiful, all hidden away,
Hidden by grass, in the meadows they stay,
Until the wind makes them dance all around,
With petals floating and touching the ground,
Like dancers they bend and sway,
Blowing in the wind, they flutter and play,
They swirl and twirl one more time,
Tiny, yellow dancers spring around.

Isobel Eddy (7)
Radyr Primary School, Cardiff

The Soft Badger

The badger is soft like a kitten
His fur is soft like a dog
He sleeps in the day and he goes out a night
When somebody shouts it gives him a fright
His eyes are like shiny, little marbles.
I love animals.

Rebecca Bunney (9)
Radyr Primary School, Cardiff

Dogs

Dogs are big,
Dogs are small,
Dogs are round,
Dogs are tall,
I saw a dog sitting on a wall,
I saw a dog wearing a crown,
I saw a dog that was brown.

Christina Berry (9)
Radyr Primary School, Cardiff

Summer

Summer looks like a beach
Full of children laughing,
Splashing in the deep, blue sea.
Summer tastes like dinner
Sizzling on the barbecue,
Summer sounds like the waves
Crashing against the rocks.
Summer feels like bluebells
Tickling my legs.
Summer smells like daisies, bluebells.

Daniel Oglesby (9)
St Therese's School, Port Talbot

Spring

Spring is flowers in the meadow, lambs have just been born.
Spring is birds singing as they fly along.
Spring is feeling happy, playing with joy.
Spring tastes like Easter eggs on the holy day.
Spring smells like daisies and buttercups too.
I love spring, I hope you do too?

Leah Emery (8)
St Therese's School, Port Talbot

Summer

Children building castles
In the golden sand.
Hanging baskets trailing bright flowers.
Bathing under sapphire skies.
Summer sounds of tweeting birds.
Beef sizzling on the barbecue.
Feeling hot and happy.
Eating hot, tasty, barbecued chicken.
Smell flowers in the green, breezy field.

Travis Monks Landeg (8)
St Therese's School, Port Talbot

Summer

Splashing waves in the sea.
Children playing on the hot sand.
Birds singing sweetly in the sky.
People laughing loudly.
Cold suncream on your hot body.
Sand sticking on wet bathers.
Licking sweet, dripping ice lollies.
Smell the sizzling barbecue.

Hannah Piles (9)
St Therese's School, Port Talbot

Summer

It looks like a crowded beach.
Sounds like the waves are fighting.
Feels like the breeze is tackling you.
Tastes like a juicy peach.
Smells like bluebells and buttercups.

Kalon Smithers (8)
St Therese's School, Port Talbot

Summer

Summer looks like small, tiny birds in a cherry blossom tree.
That's what summer looks like.

Summer sounds like blue waves
splashing against the sharp, grey rocks.
That's what summer sounds like.

Summer feels like hot air in our faces
and the blazing hot sun shining.
That's what summer feels like.

Summer tastes like cold strawberries in thick creamy cream
and freezing ice cubes in a glass of Coke.
Now that's what summer tastes like.

Summer smells like meaty, fat, chewy beef burgers
cooking on burnt charcoal.
That's definitely what summer smells like.

Bethan Maund (9)
St Therese's School, Port Talbot

Summer

Daisies blowing back and forth
In the gentle breeze.
The blue sky glowing.
Birds singing sweetly
With their lovely voices.

Cold drinks with ice cubes and lemon.
Cold chocolate, tasty ice cream with a flake.
Sitting on the beach catching a tan.
Jumping in the sea.
Fatty burgers on the barbecue
With a sizzling noise.

Carly Green (9)
St Therese's School, Port Talbot

Summer

On the beach the blazing hot sun shining.
Daisies blowing in the cool breeze.

See the tanned people posing.
Turquoise sea splashing.

Bees buzzing in the air.
Dolphins jumping.
That's what summer sounds like.

Having a cool drink in the hot sun.
Pineapples, apples and pears to eat.
That's what summer feels like.

Duck cooking on the barbecue,
Burgers and sausages.
That's what summer tastes like.

Benjamin Jack Potts (8)
St Therese's School, Port Talbot

Summer

Summer is Heaven.
Bluebells in the field.
Warm breeze blowing in the air.
Blossoms waving.
Scarlet-red roses blooming.
The sun shining on me.
Barbecues blazing hot.
Fat, sizzling sausages.
The morning sky spreads a rosy light.
Creamy ice cream, cold and fresh
Dripping in the hot sun.

Emilie Potts (8)
St Therese's School, Port Talbot

Summer

Blue sparkling water.
Golden-yellow sand.
Waves crashing into the rocks.

Birds tweeting in the trees.
Children talking to their friends.

It's hot with that gleaming, yellow diamond in the sky.
The deep blue sea is very warm.

Hot dogs on the barbecue.
Cold, icy drinks.
The nice smell of the buttercups and daisies.

Luke Ball (9)
St Therese's School, Port Talbot

Summer

The sun is bright and the barbecue's tonight.
The sky is a beautiful blue.
Golden buttercups and daises crowd the fields.
Picnics on the beach.
Happy faces.
Long, lazy days.

Joshua Michael Ready (9)
St Therese's School, Port Talbot

Summer

Flapping birds in the sweet, blue sky.
Delicious vanilla ice cream.
Smell the red, juicy strawberries.
Beautiful blossoms.

Dominic Bamsey (9)
St Therese's School, Port Talbot

Winter

Snow on the window sill, snow in the street.
That's what winter looks like.
Snow on the rooftops, snow in the chimney.
That's what winter looks like.

Wind blowing gently through the house.
That's what winter sounds like.
Hailstones crashing down to the ground.
That's what winter sounds like.

A giant turkey cooking in the oven.
That's what winter tastes like.
A hot apple pie burning in your mouth.
That's what winter tastes like.

Jack Ormond Lewis (8)
St Therese's School, Port Talbot

Summer

Blazing sun in a diamond-blue sky.
Sweet perfume of beautiful, red roses.
Gentle breeze in the hot sun.
Ice cream melting in the hot sun.
Bees buzzing in my ear.
Birds singing to wake me.

Abigail May Jones (9)
St Therese's School, Port Talbot

Autumn

Golden, crispy leaves floating down.
Wind howling like wolves, rustling in the trees.

Pumpkins, big and orange, glowing with scary faces.
Bonfire smoke clouding the night sky.

Robert Morgan (9)
St Therese's School, Port Talbot

Dragon Poem

Dragons are scaly,
Dragons have gigantic wings.
A dragon is red.

A dragon is loud,
Dragons roar very loudly,
Dragons sound scary.

Dragons feel scaly,
Dragons are very spiky,
Dragons are bumpy.

Dragons breathe out fire,
A dragon frightens people,
Dragons guard castles.

Megan Williams (7)
Tredegarville Primary School, Cardiff

The Dragon

Dragon breathing hot fire,
Flying in the deep blue sky,
Red, huge wings flapping in the moonlight,
Swooping in the light village,
Eating and tearing people's skin,
Scary dragon out at night,
Red dragon scaring the little children away,
The dragon roars as loud as people screaming.
Dragon out at night, beware.

Marie Chambers (9)
Tredegarville Primary School, Cardiff

Dragon Poem

A dragon has fangs,
Dragons are really scary,
Dragons are so strong.

Dragons roar loudly,
Dragons have frightening roars,
Dragons sound scary.

A dragon is rough,
A dragon is leathery,
Dragons are spiky.

Dragons are naughty,
A dragon frightens people,
Dragons fight with knights.

Shannon-Leigh Evans (8)
Tredegarville Primary School, Cardiff

The Dragon

The sight of a hungry, nasty dragon.
The sound of cracking bones.

Crack!
Crash!
Snap!

The smell of fire burning.
The taste of bubbling bones and blood.
The feeling of darkness.

Going into his dark, scary cave.

Atlanta Hewings (8)
Tredegarville Primary School, Cardiff

The Dragon

The sight of a hungry, gigantic, ugly dragon.
The sound of cracking, cooking bones.
The smell of fire burning.
The taste of burning ashes.
The feeling of a dragon coming up to you and
Snap!
You've been eaten by a dragon!

Natasha Wilkinson (8)
Tredegarville Primary School, Cardiff

The Dragon

The sight of a horrible, scary, mean dragon
With eyes as big as stones.
The sound of a roaring dragon, so scary.
The smell of smoke, fire breath.
The taste of crunchy bones and buildings.
The feeling of people crying, 'Help!'
And lots of screaming.

Ross O'Connell (9)
Tredegarville Primary School, Cardiff

The Dragon

Dragon, dragon, what do you seek?
Dragon, dragon, how do you peek?
Dragon, dragon, where do you hide?
Dragon, dragon, were you asleep?
Dragon, dragon, can you snore?
Dragon, dragon, go to sleep.

Kyle Ellaway (9)
Tredegarville Primary School, Cardiff